From Palestine
to America

From Palestine
to America

◆

A Memoir

Taher Dajani

iUniverse, Inc.
New York Bloomington Shanghai

From Palestine to America
A Memoir

Copyright © 2008 by Taher Dajani

iUniverse books may be ordered through booksellers or by contacting:

iUniverse
1663 Liberty Drive
Bloomington, IN 47403
www.iuniverse.com
1-800-Authors (1-800-288-4677)

Because of the dynamic nature of the Internet, any Web addresses or links contained in this book may have changed since publication and may no longer be valid.

The views expressed in this work are solely those of the author and do not necessarily reflect the views of the publisher, and the publisher hereby disclaims any responsibility for them.

ISBN: 978-0-595-48286-3 (pbk)
ISBN: 978-0-595-71784-2 (cloth)
ISBN: 978-0-595-60373-2 (ebk)

Printed in the United States of America

This book is dedicated to the memory of my parents
and to Sheila, Amira and Zena.

Contents

Old City of Jaffa

Poem
Bride of the Sea

I was very much in love
I couldn't sleep
I left her in total exhaustion
On a black boat sailing without a flag
Waves in turmoil all around it
The passengers incredulous, regretful

I left the lights of Jaffa dying behind me
The dreams of youth scattered in the air
I promised I would come back to her
With open arms and yearning
I am very much in love
With Jaffa the Bride of the Sea

—TD

Bride of the Sea (Arabic)

عروس البحر

أنا في هواها لم أنمْ
وغادرتها ليلاً بحالِ عدمْ
على شراعٍ أسودٍ مبحرٍ بلا علمْ
ووجه البحر مضطربٌ والركاب في ندمْ

رأيت أضواء يافا ساكنةً ورائي
وأحلام الصبا تناثرت في الهواءِ
قلت لها هاتفاً عروس البحر إني
راجعٌ لك رجعةَ الولهانِ

—TD

BRIDE OF THE SEA

Violin

Taher Dajani

Prologue

For forty-six years I dreamed of going back to Palestine, the land my family had been forced to flee in 1948 to escape the onslaught of the Zionist militias that had encircled Jaffa. In 1994 my wish came true when I was sent on an International Monetary Fund assignment to Israel, the West Bank, and Gaza. At the end of my official business I traveled by road from Jerusalem to Jaffa, the place of my birth, to search for my roots and to see again the house where I grew up.

With sadness I saw that our house and the surrounding homes, many belonging to relatives, had been demolished. I went to a nearby restaurant in the hopes of finding out what had happened. Bulldozers had roared into the neighborhood, the houses were turned into rubble, and pushed down the hill into the Mediterranean. The State of Israel now holds the resulting wide space of prime land. I sat in the restaurant trying to contain my anger and disappointment before going to look for our orange grove on the outskirts of the city. The grove had been inherited by my father and had been in our family for many years. I was stunned to find it had completely gone, together with all the surrounding orange groves. The area was filled with apartment buildings, all occupied by Jewish families.

My mind went back to the days when I was growing up and to the events that led to our exodus from Jaffa and the hardships and successes we experienced during our exile from Palestine. I knew that one day I would write down my thoughts and describe my journey from Palestine to America.

1

Jaffa

Jaffa is considered one of the oldest seaports in the world. It was called Yafi by the ancient Canaanites, which means the beautiful. The city is referred to as Yafa in Arabic, Yafo in Hebrew, Yoppa in Greek and Yapu in Egyptian inscriptions. It is the City of Oranges and the Bride of the Sea. Throughout its history of over 4,000 years Jaffa saw many invaders including Egyptians, Israelites, Assyrians, Babylonians, Phoenicians, Persians, Greeks, Romans, Arabs, Turks and French. Sadly Jaffa is now part of Israel.

My family roots in Jaffa (Yafa), Palestine go back to Sheikh Saleem al-Dajani (1759–1839). He descended from Sheikh Ahmad (1498–1561) who lived in Dajania, later known as Djania (El Jania) or D'gania, a village near Jerusalem. Sheikh Ahmad's ancestors are traced back to Sayeda Fatima the daughter of the Prophet Mohammad. Sheikh Ahmad was buried in Jerusalem. Other sources have it that the name Dajani could have been derived from Beit Dajan, a village about 6 miles east of Jaffa referred to in the bible as Dagon. According to this version of our history the family roots date back to the Canaanites, who inhabited the land of milk and honey before the invasion of the Israelites from Egypt.

Sheikh Saleem was a graduate of al Azhar University in Cairo, Egypt. Al Azhar is considered the chief center of Islamic and Arabic learning in the world. Its basic program of studies was, and still is, Islamic Law, theology and the Arabic language. He had a wide knowledge of Shari'a (Islamic Law) and Sufism (the articulation of the idea of a path by which the true believer could draw nearer to God). Sheikh Saleem was appointed the Mufti of Jaffa—the highest religious authority that interprets and expounds on matters related to the Islamic law—and he had homes in

Jaffa and Beit Dajan. One of Saleem's contributions to Palestinian history was that during the Napoleonic invasion of Jaffa, Saleem, together with the scion of the Damiani family who acted as consul for Italy and whose Christian ancestors go back to the crusades, went to meet Napoleon to ask him to spare the lives of the Jaffa garrison that surrendered, undertaking to provide for them. At that time Napoleon's army killed more than 2,500 captive Muslim fighters allegedly because food supplies were barely sufficient for the invading troops. Family records tell us that Napoleon heeded the request. The Napoleonic invasion was aborted when his troops could not breach the walls of the northern city of Acre and as his army was hit by the plague.

Saleem's son Hussein (1787–1858) and his brothers (Muhammad and Hassan) studied Arabic grammar, literature and religion under their father and were sent to Cairo, Egypt to study in al-Azhar. Hussein became well known for his teachings and publications, and in 1820 was appointed the Mufti of Jaffa. At the age of seventy-two he traveled with his brother Hassan and his cousin Abu Rabah al Dajani to Mecca for the Hajj. He died and was buried there.[1]

His brother Hassan (1816–1890) my great, great, grandfather was also well known as a scholar and like his brother was appointed Mufti of Jaffa. In his book, Hiliat al Bashar in the Thirteenth Hijri Century (Wholesome Personalities in the 19th Century) published in Arabic in 1961 by The Council of Arabic Linguists in Damascus, Sheikh Abd al Razik al Bitar mentioned both Hussein and Hassan as learned and highly respected with a wide knowledge of Arabic literature and Islamic law. He added that their ancestry goes back to the Prophet Muhammad and that their presence, kindness and humility were exemplary. He also highlighted the contributions of Abu Rabah al Dajani and Ali Abu al Mawahib, the son of Hussein. Both were well known Sufis renowned for their generosity and charitable giving to the poor.

From here on the letters al (meaning the) preceding the family name will be omitted.

The Dajanis lived in the old city of Jaffa, which sits on a rocky hill overlooking the Mediterranean from three sides: West, North and South. The port was nestled down below the steep western side, on which lay two- and three-story houses, clustered around narrow roads and alleys and connected by winding stone stairs.

A high wall and a moat encircled the old city to protect it from invading armies. By 1888, in order to expand the city, the wall was completely dismantled and the moat covered with earth. New roads opened north and south and new suburbs sprang up. It was at this time that my great-grandfather, Sheikh Ali Fouz, his brother and cousins built homes in the Ajami quarter a mile south of the old city on a high plateau overlooking the sea. The first local hospital, built in Jaffa at the beginning of the 19th Century by the Ottomans, was on land in the Ajami quarter donated by Ali Fouz. At that time there were only a few hospitals in the city, which were owned and operated by Christian missionaries.

My grandfather Sheikh Mahmoud (1864–1936), like several of his cousins, was educated at home and in traditional schools before going for higher education in Arabic literature and Islamic studies at al Azhar in Cairo. After graduation he served as a judge in Palestine, Syria and Libya under the Ottoman Administration. He was married to Fatima Bakri, my grandmother, whose family came from Hebron, Palestine. She was knowledgeable in religious matters and the Dajani women sought after her advice. She bore three children: Abdelkareem, Ishaq and Tayeb (my father). Abdelkareem, like his father studied at al Azhar in Cairo, but died a few years after graduation from typhoid fever in Horan, Syria where my grandfather was posted. Ishaq did not go to university and did administrative work in law offices and dabbled in real estate. He married Fakhriya Bakri, his first cousin but had no children.

Six Generations of the Dajani Family

Saleem (1759–1839)

———

Hussein, Mohammad, Hassan (1816–1890)

———

Arif, Ragheb, Mustafa, Adib Pasha, Ali fouz (1841–1910)

———

Ragheb, Abdel Ghani, Muhammad, Mahmoud (1864–1936)

———

Abdelkarim, Ishaq, Tayeb (1907–1985)

———

Mahmoud, Taher, Sidqi, Salwa, Khawla

My father, Tayeb, studied at Rashidiya College in Jerusalem, established in 1914 by the Ottoman Turkish Administration and at the American University of Beirut, Lebanon, together with several of his cousins. Other cousins went to study in Britain, France and Germany. This was a major departure from the religious education acquired by most of their forebears that had put them in a special place of influence as Ulama or learned men during the Ottoman administration.

My father while a student at AUB in Beirut

My father cut his studies short and took a teaching job. He got married at the age of twenty-one to Subhia Jabri who was seventeen years old and whose grandfather, Ata Jabri, had come from Damascus, Syria in 1871 to set up an import/export business. Ata became a successful merchant and owned several properties in Jaffa. Because of his wide contacts the Persian Government appointed him as an honorary consul in Palestine. Recently, a friend of the family told us at a dinner party that when he was young he was asked to contribute money to a worthy cause. He could not afford to pay much and justified this by using a common phrase prevalent at that time "I am not the son of Ata Jabri" who was noted for his affluence and generosity. Most of Ata's wealth was lost after his death as a result of unsuccessful trade deals and careless spending by his sons Anees, Ibraheem and Ahmad. Ata also had a daughter, Zeinab. Ibraheem was my maternal grandfather. He was married to Salwa al Bahri from Damascus and they had two sons, Khalil and Ali, and three daughters, Fawzia, Adiba, and Subhia (my mother).

Uncle Ishaq was on the look out for a suitable wife for his brother Tayeb. On a visit to Ali Jabri he saw Subhia in passing and thought she would be a good match for Tayeb. After talking it over with his parents and with Tayeb it was agreed that he would broach the subject with Ali, who welcomed the idea. After that my grandfather went to officially ask for Subhia's hand from her elder brother Khalil, who was her guardian after their father's death of natural causes in his late 60's.

The wedding took place in our house in Jaffa and was attended by a large number of relatives and friends. We are told that, as was the custom then, Tayeb was carried on the shoulders of his friends and relatives for the Zaffeh (wedding celebration) where music was played while his friends sang of his attributes, in the streets of the neighborhood before entering the house. Subhia who was brought to the house by her mother and sisters sat on a high chair, like a throne, fully made up and surrounded by ladies who were invited and who sang and danced for the occasion. After the celebration Tayeb and Subhia, who met for the first time that evening, were escorted to their bedroom in the big house.

Subhia (my mother) bore seven children: four boys and two girls. The boys are Mahmoud who died in infancy, Mahmoud Mahasen, Taher, (the author) and Sidqi. The girls are Salwa and Khawla. My grandfather suggested compound names for the three boys, shown on their birth certificates as Mahmoud Mahasen, Mohammad Taher and Ahmad Sidqi.

At the beginning of their marriage my father, beside his teaching job, supervised the production and marketing of the orange crop at the grove in Jabaliya, about a mile from Ajami quarter. A few years later he engaged in the cement trade and tile manufacturing, neither of which proved successful, mainly because of unrest under British rule, which had begun in 1918 following the defeat in World War I of the Ottoman Empire under which the Arab countries, with varying degrees, lived for centuries.

The history of British rule began in 1916 when Sharif Hussein of Mecca declared the Arab Revolt against the Ottoman Turks. He was backed by Britain, which promised to support the creation of an Arab kingdom based in Damascus. However, the British Government had other objectives in the area and a hidden agenda. In 1917 it issued the Balfour Declaration supporting a Jewish national homeland in Palestine and in 1918, after the War was won, the Allies reneged on their promise and carved up the Middle East. The League of Nations confirmed British mandates over Iraq and Palestine, and a French mandate over Syria and Lebanon. Transjordan was separated from the Palestine Mandate and became an autonomous kingdom.[2]

Palestine under the British Mandate, 1923-1948

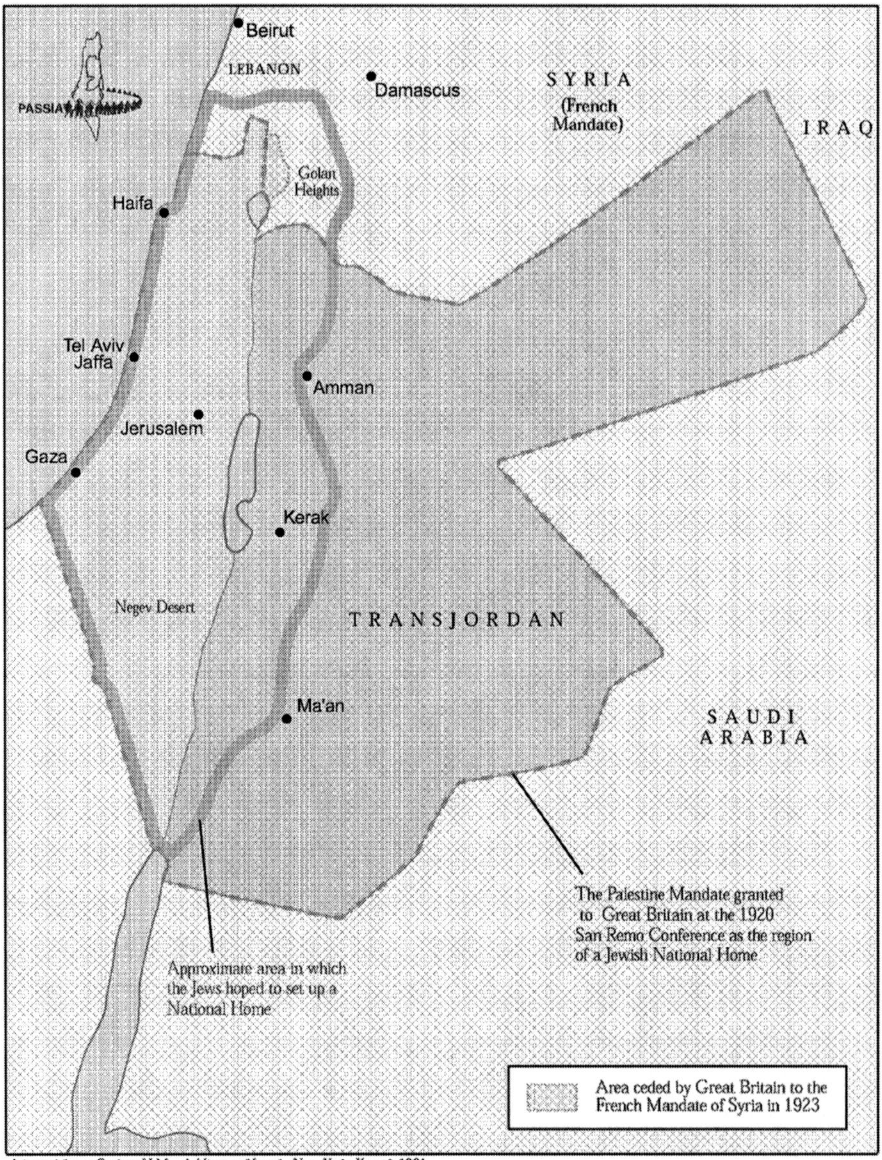

Beirut

LEBANON

Damascus

SYRIA
(French
Mandate)

IRAQ

PASSIA

Golan
Heights

Haifa

Tel Aviv
Jaffa

Amman

Jerusalem

Gaza

Kerak

Negev Desert

TRANSJORDAN

Ma'an

SAUDI
ARABIA

The Palestine Mandate granted
to Great Britain at the 1920
San Remo Conference as the region
of a Jewish National Home

Approximate area in which
the Jews hoped to set up a
National Home

Area ceded by Great Britain to the
French Mandate of Syria in 1923

Adapted from: Sachar, H.M., A History of Israel, New York: Knopf, 1981

Source: Palestinian Academic Society for the Study of International
Affairs (PASSIA), Jerusalem. Reprinted with permission of PASSIA.

The flow of Jewish emigrants into Palestine accelerated in the twenties and the thirties and became a major concern to the Palestinians, both Moslems and Christians. To maintain sectarian harmony and guard against the British policy of divide and rule, the first Islamic Christian society was founded in 1918 under the chairmanship of Sheikh Ragheb Abu Saud Dajani, the Islamic Shari'a Judge of Jaffa. In 1921 and 1929 the Arabs rioted in Jaffa and throughout Palestine, and in 1935 Sheikh Izz el-Din al-Qassam was killed by British troops as he led a major armed uprising. In 1936 major unrest and a general strike started in Jaffa and spread all over the country. Armed attacks by the local population against the Jews and the British gained momentum and the Palestinian fighters temporarily took control of major cities, but by 1939 the British, with cooperation from the Haganaha, a Jewish militia, put down the revolt with stern measures, including the demolition of villages and parts of Jaffa. They also used Arab civilians as human shields against attacks by armed bands[3]. Zionist settlers uprooted Arabs from D'gania, the village where my forebears once lived, and transferred them to other villages as part of the Zionist colonization process.[4]

Both my uncle and my father were active in the resistance. My father's brother, Uncle Ishaq, was incarcerated for six months at Atleit prison near the city of Acre and my father took refuge in Beirut, Lebanon, for fear of being arrested. He stayed with one of his cousins, Kamel Dajani, who escaped earlier. Kamel (the future father-in-law of my brother Sidqi) was the owner of a newspaper in Jaffa and an active member of the Palestinian Arab Party. Both returned to Jaffa a few months later when the wave of arrests quieted down. The fortunes of most of the Dajanis dwindled during British rule because of their active opposition to British occupation and policy, unlike during the time when Palestine was a province of the Ottoman Empire. The Dajanis had thrived then by virtue of their position as Ulama (learned religious men).

I remember the times we went by bus with Aunt Fakhriya to Atleit Prison to visit my uncle. I also remember the morning my father left for Beirut camouflaged as a port laborer. He walked down the hill from our house to the beach and walked north to the port where he met with friends who helped him get on a boat going to Lebanon. I ran after him crying and asking to go with him. He gently took me back to the house and promised to return quickly. My mother who remained calm wiped my tears and tried to comfort me. Other memories come to mind. Because of unrest in Jaffa, fueled by British policy in Palestine, British soldiers, with rifles on their shoulders, used to patrol our neighborhood at different times of the day, much to the resentment of our people. They walked together in groups of four. My father told me in later years that one afternoon I was with him at the grocery store near our house. When the soldiers passed I cursed them in Arabic expressing my anger at their presence in the neighborhood. I was five or six years old.

Our neighborhood in Jaffa was mixed with Muslims and Christians living together in harmony. There were no Jewish families in our neighborhood since they had their own colonies around Jaffa where no Arabs lived. The midwife who delivered my siblings and me was Christian by the name of Alia Modawar. My brothers and I used to regularly visit a Christian neighbor who assisted an ophthalmologist downtown to treat our eyes with special eye drops to prevent the eye disease trachoma. The eye drops caused a sharp burning sensation that made us dread the next round of treatment, but we dreaded more contracting trachoma. Our neighborhood soccer (football) team, of which I was a member, was also mixed and often played matches against other neighborhood teams. Soccer was the national sport of Palestine. I used to go with other players to watch the major clubs in town (e.g., the Islamic Club and the Orthodox Club) play against each other or against clubs from other cities. Jerusalem boasted major soccer clubs, one of which was the Dajani Club. A close relative, Nader Dajani, whose father was a civil judge in Jaffa, played on the team. Nader recently passed away in Washington, D.C.

Boxing was also popular and I loved the sport and played matches with the neighborhood children. I was thirteen years old. When I was younger I boxed with brother Mahmoud at home. We wrapped towels around our hands, locked the door and boxed until we were exhausted. For practice, I filled a linen bag with sand, hung it in the outer yard of our house and punched it until I got tired. As part of the practice I would gently push the bag with my hand and let it come back on my nose in order to get used to real punches. I am sure this did not do my nose any good, and I dread to think about it. Adib Dasouki who came from Jaffa was one of the top boxing champions in the Middle East.

Taher in the backyard of the house

Our house had an open courtyard with a well and a raised small garden. In the middle of the courtyard a large carved wooden door led to a medium size hall, which had two doors. One door led to the Diwan (reception room) and the other led to a much larger hall. The Diwan was adorned with a burgundy velvet couch and arm chairs arranged around the room, a large square mahogany wooden table in the middle, a desk and a chair in one corner, and an His Masters Voice phonograph in another corner. A large picture of my grandfather in his formal judge's attire hung on the wall together with a picture of Uncle Abdelkareem who died in his youth. On the opposite wall hung separate pictures of Mahmoud, Sidqi and myself. Two windows overlooked the open courtyard and another two overlooked a sandy square where my friends and I used to play soccer, much to the annoyance of our relative Muneeb Dajani (Abu Racheed) whose house lay at the end of the sandy square. The large hall extended along the length of the house. The floors were covered with multi-colored tiles: light gray, black, and brick red. In the winter months Turkmani and Persian carpets were placed in the Diwan and other selected areas of the house. Sheepskin rugs were placed beside the beds in the bedrooms. In the summer the carpets were taken outside and beaten with long sticks to get rid of the dust, rolled up and placed under the beds; they were replaced by straw mats, called Hassiras, except in the Diwan, where the carpet was rolled back after cleaning.

On one side of the big hall two windows overlooked the sandy square and a long wooden doushak (bench) with fancy covers and cushions provided a sitting place near the windows. On the opposite side, which straddled the house of our relatives (Motei and Huda Dajani, Umm Fawzi) four large sky-light-windows with stained glass lay near the wooden ceiling that had ornamented frames all around it. Here in the big hall my brothers and I used to play indoor soccer using soft balls and sometimes oranges that came from our orange grove on the outskirts of town. Mother would step in to put a halt to the play particularly if my father was taking a nap in the afternoon. Along the hall lay large bedrooms that overlooked the sea. Each bedroom was furnished with modern beds, mahogany wooden closets and dressers and a doushak (bench), with fancy covers and cushions, along one wall beside the windows.

The kitchen and bathroom occupied part of the area opposite the bedrooms with a dining table and chairs placed in between. At the left side corner of the hallway lay an entry that led to an old bathroom and to the open courtyard. Two large carved and polished wooden cupboards and an icebox stood on the wall between the second and third bedroom. Every morning 2 large ice blocks were delivered to the house to keep the icebox cold. At one time the dining table was round with short legs and we sat cross-legged around it to eat. Later it was replaced with a modern high table and chairs.

ساهر الدجاني

Taher in 1947 at age 13

All the bed mattresses were stuffed with wool and occasionally a Munajjed (an upholsterer) would come to the house, take the mattresses out to the courtyard, empty each of its stuffing and fluff up the wool with a special instrument that he carried with him. After leaving the wool in the sun for a while he would refill the mattresses and sew them up again. The laundry process was labor intensive. The clothes were boiled in a dist (tin bath), with the white wash first soaked in Zahra (washing blue). Every piece was then scrubbed by hand, wrung out and placed to dry on washing lines in the outer courtyard.

At the end of the open courtyard a room was built to accommodate a family friend (Murad) and his two young children (Mustapha and Atef). Murad's mother was a close friend of my grandmother who had helped Murad find a wife. Unfortunately, the wife died early and left Murad with the two boys. My grandmother took pity on the young man and asked him to move to our house so that the children would be taken care of.

Later as the children grew up, Murad's family moved out. The room and the space near it were then used to raise pigeons for eating. Stuffed pigeons were a delicacy. Both Mustapha and Atef quit elementary school and found jobs to help their father who was a carpenter. At times Atef went near the port area and ran after trucks loaded with sugar, jumped on the truck, reached for the closest sack, tore a line in it with a razor blade, and as the sugar started to seep out he positioned his own linen bag under it until it was full and then he jumped out. He sold the sugar, which was expensive, to grocery stores. One day I saw this happening and told my father about it. He immediately warned Murad. If Atef had been caught, the police would have come down hard on him.

Originally the house had neither electricity nor city water. Our drinking water was brought up from the well in the courtyard to a tank and then pumped up to another tank on the roof by Yousef, a blind young man from Jabal Duruz in Syria who lived nearby. For light we used kerosene lamps. Later, both city water and electricity were brought in and an icebox was purchased. The neighborhood children loved our cold water after a soccer game in the hot summer sun. During the British mandate public utilities, health facilities, the transportation system and educational institutions were modernized.

The roof of the house was brick in the middle over the hall and flat concrete over the other parts. Our family was large. Beside my parents, two brothers and two sisters, there were my grandmother, Uncle Ishaq and his wife Fakhria, Fatima Basheer who joined our family at a young age, and a maid called Mariam. Fatima was an orphan from Jericho who lived in Jaffa with her uncle and aunt. One evening on their way home from a picnic at our orange grove my family saw Fatima standing near the entrance, anxiety and fear on her pretty young face. My mother asked her about her parents and their address and was told that her parents passed away sometime ago in Jericho and her uncle had brought her to Jaffa to live with his family. Fatima did not want to go back to her uncle because he did not take good care of her, and his wife continuously punished her and pushed her around. She beseeched my mother to let her work and live in our house. It was getting dark and my mother felt the young girl could not be left alone.

So Fatima, who was about 15 years old, came home with the family. She assisted my mother in daily household chores and helped with the children.

I remember when my brothers and I went with Fatima downtown to the photographer and to the cinema. We took Bus No. 1., which had a stop near the house. We went to see Egyptian films, like Dumou el Hub (Tears of Love), Youm Said (A Happy Day), and Alwarda al Beida (The White Rose). Jaffa cinemas also offered the latest Hollywood releases. Fatima loved to sing and did her jobs in the house while singing the latest hits. At the age of twenty she left our house to work for a British family. She met Mohammad Abdel Rahman, from the Sudan, who worked as a cook for the British military in Jaffa. They got married and had a daughter whom they named Bashira. Eventually Bashira was adopted into our family and became a sister to us all. I remember Abdel Rahman from his frequent visits with Fatima to our family. He was tall, handsome and jovial with shining black skin and long beauty scars on both cheeks. A year later Fatima and her husband separated and then divorced. Fatima came to stay in our house with the baby. Some time after that Abdel Rahman went back to the Sudan and Fatima married an older man by the name of Abdu Shatara.

My brothers and I attended Annahda Islamic Elementary School, a private school financed by the Awqaf (Islamic Trust), a religious endowment in Islam typically devoting a land or a building for religious or charitable purposes. The principal and one of the teachers were relatives of ours. I did very well the first three years but started to lag because I was more interested in playing soccer. I had private lessons in mathematics but most of the time my mind during the sessions spaced out in the direction of the soccer field and my friends. I was very active and energetic and hated to sit still for too long. The principal of the school, Hamdi Dajani, told my father at that time that my training in future years should be vocational because I was not studious, but my father had a different view.

After graduating from elementary school my brothers and I attended Amiriya Secondary School, which had a modern curriculum and a commerce section for those who wanted to specialize in bookkeeping and secretarial work. The British authorities approved the curriculum of all government schools. The principal of Amiriya was Ali Shaath, a graduate of the American University of Beirut. Two of the teachers were Hafez Dajani, also a graduate of the AUB who taught business courses, and Said Dajani, a graduate of Rashidiya College in Jerusalem, who taught Arabic, both of whom were third cousins of my father.

My father (left) with Hamdi Dajani

Hamdi and Jawad Dajani, another relative, used to stop by our house in the late afternoons to pick up my father and walk to Hmeid Cafe' close by where they met with several other Dajanis, including Hafez, in the outdoors overlooking the Mediterranean, or indoors in the winter months, to play backgammon and talk about the news of the day. A special area was reserved for them in the cafe'. Coffee was served as a matter of course.

Spending the afternoons in cafes (for men at least) is still a popular pastime all over the Middle East.

My father was an avid reader and was fond of geography and Arabic poetry. He used to gather us around him and quiz us on the capitals of countries starting from the obvious and going gradually to the more difficult, such as Mongolia and Finland. Then he would go into poetry reciting a line from a poem and asking us to match the last letter in the line with the first letter of another poem line.

In the summer months, on Friday mornings and holidays my father took us to the Ajami Beach Club, within walking distance of our house, where we met with relatives. Next to our beach club was the British Officers Club, which was relatively fancy. Both British men and women swam and surfed together, unlike our club where only men went to swim in public. In the afternoons the officers and their wives and girl friends came from town in droves, driving their private and military vehicles that filled both sides of the street leading to the club. A diving board was fixed to a large steel chair, which was anchored down to a flat rock that extended far into the sea. I, with other kids, used to watch from a distance the British diving. Only members were allowed into the Club and its swimming area. In 1947–48 as the British troops started to leave Palestine the club was closed. Only then were we able to use the beach and the diving area. The waters in both beaches were protected somewhat by rocks that extended into the sea quite a distance on both sides. In low tide we walked on the rocks to catch small crabs and fish. Discovering new rock pools was thrilling for me. The individual pools were washed clean every day as the tide came in. Then as the tide went out they were left with shining, transparent water teeming with little fish. I loved to clamber over the rocks and fish in the pools.

One day I and a playmate from the neighborhood, whose father owned the Ajami Beach Club, took a hasaka (a flat surf boat) and went out of sight all the way to the big ships standing outside the port. It was scary and caused a lot of anxiety on the part of our parents when they realized we were missing. Also on the same beach I once hit my head on the rocks smack in the middle as I was riding the waves. Now, with my hair thinning I can clearly see the scars in the mirror. Another scar that I acquired in my youth is on my forehead. Some afternoons we went on picnics to the orange grove. We used to climb the tall mulberry tree to pick mulberries and swim in the pool, which was used for irrigation. Diving in a shallow area I split open my forehead. Luckily, the bleeding stopped quickly by pressing a linen cloth over the wound. The family afternoon picnic was ruined. If it hadn't been for our troubles with the British and the Zionist Jews my childhood could be considered idyllic at least until I was 14 years old. I was surrounded by a loving family, lived in a picturesque town by the sea with a delightful climate. Looking back on my happy days "messing about in boats", playing soccer, going on picnics, I feel blessed. If only it could have continued.

My grandmother tutored my mother in Quranic verses and sayings of the prophet. In the early days whenever one of us fell ill my grandmother put her palm on one's forehead and read prayers asking God for a quick recovery. My mother followed the practice. When Bells Palsy hit me in my adulthood and caused my mouth to droop to one side, she placed under my pillow the white prayer skullcap of our ancestor Hussein Dajani who was a renowned Sofi scholar and recited several Suras from the Quran while sitting on my bed.

How much of my recovery was due to the B-12 vitamin injections or the blessings of my mother cannot be ascertained with confidence. Both went hand in hand, I would say. Two of my relatives who were later hit by Bells Palsy developed a crooked mouth and never recovered.

When my brothers and I started a bad cough my grandmother, with the help of mother, brought out of the cupboard the famous glass cups (Cassat al Hawa, which means air cups) to apply on our backs. A strip of newspaper was wound around, lit with a match and placed in the cup. With the flame rising they placed the cup on our back to suck the chill from our system. As the air in the cup became hot it created a suction mechanism, which held the cup tightly in place until it was removed. Warm olive oil was then applied on the area of operation. At one time my chest cold was severe, so after removing the cups from my back the now crimson skin that was under the cup was cut with a razor blade to release some blood. I still have the scars on my back. How effective a remedy that was remains to be researched.

My mother had an amiable personality, a high level of common sense, and a strong will. She and my aunt Fakhria worked together amicably taking turns in preparing the meals and kneading the dough and rolling it into flat loaves. Fresh bread was made every day. Other chores like cleaning and washing clothes were left for the maid. A delivery boy from the neighborhood bakery came in mid-morning to collect the unbaked loaves from our house, which in the neighborhood was called Beit al Qadi (the judge's house) and he would try to come back with the hot bread before lunch. In case of delay one of us boys would go to the bakery to hurry up matters. Sometimes, open-faced meat pies would be laid on a large heavy platter for the delivery boy to also take to the bakery. He carried the platter on his head, which was covered with a thick cloth turban wound in such a way as to make a platform.

My mother was a marvelous cook and produced delicious meals, often from the simplest ingredients. A few cups of flour, a little water and butter, ground-meat, onions and spices and an hour later a wonderful batch of the safiha (small pastries stuffed with meat) was ready to go to the bakery. These would be eaten with yogurt on the side. The marketing was done almost every day with my father often bringing home from the neighborhood grocery fruit, vegetables, sugar, flour, and from the butcher lamb cuts, kidneys and sheep brains. Sometimes, the maid would step over to the grocery or the butcher shop to get what was needed quickly. The shops were across the street from the house.

All fresh food was washed very carefully. Meat was well cooked usually with vegetables such as green beans, peas, tomatoes, and the resulting stew was always exceedingly tasty. Other favorites were stuffed grape leaves and squash and kibbeh. Fresh fish from the abundant supply of the Mediterranean was served fried or as Sayyadieh (fish with rice) with tahina sauce on the side. We were also very fond of "mezza", the various dips and salads the Palestinians and Lebanese are famous for. These include hummus (chickpeas), mutabbal or babaganouj (eggplant) and tabbouli (parsley and bulgar wheat). Except for the first years as refugees, every day my mother produced a feast for us. Much of the cooking was done on simple equipment, mainly Primus kerosene portable stoves, and later on stoves operated by bottled gas.

Sweets, of which my mother was very fond, must not be forgotten. Using a drinking glass as her only measuring tool she would whip up a cake or a batch of almond cookies, which were mouth watering. Baklava was ordered from bakeries and not usually made at home. Kinafa (a layer of shredded wheat, ricotta cheese and topped with shredded wheat and honey) and mihallabiyya (a milk pudding) were often made and once again my mother excelled at making them.

My mother was very elegant and she took care of my father's wardrobe. She bought his shirts and ties for him and helped him choose his suits and shoes. She held monthly receptions for the wives of relatives and close family friends. The women visited with each other, played music (oud, tabla and daff), sang and danced. Women did not mix with men socially and like most men at that time had little schooling. They were mostly veiled (a light black head cover with a see-through face cover) whenever they went out. They had little opportunity to swim during the day. Some evenings in the moonlight my mother and some of our neighborhood relatives with their young children went down the hill to the beach and swam in pools of water protected by a long rock barrier, keeping on the long slip worn under their dresses. The glitter of lights on the horizon from felukas (small boats) that sailed out in the afternoon to catch sardines was striking. I loved to go fishing and crabbing with my brother Mahmoud near the house. Neighborhood kids with the help of their relatives fashioned small boats out of steel drums and used them for pleasure rides in calm waters. I often borrowed one of the boats with paddles and went about in high tide over the reefs.

Mother was nationalistic and was a keen observer of domestic and international political events. When President Roosevelt died in 1945 she relayed the news to us and commented on how the Allies prevailed in the war against Germany. When in 1947 Britain handed over the problem of Palestine to the UN she was full of anxiety about the outcome and when in November of that year the UN General Assembly voted to partition

Palestine into a Jewish and Arab state, with Jerusalem as an international city, mother was incredulous and angry. The Jews, who made up only one third of the population at that time and owned only 6 percent of the land, were to occupy more than half of Palestine, including the fertile coastal strip. Immediately after the partition plan was announced a general strike was declared and fighting broke out.

Landownership in Palestine and the UN Partition Plan, 1947

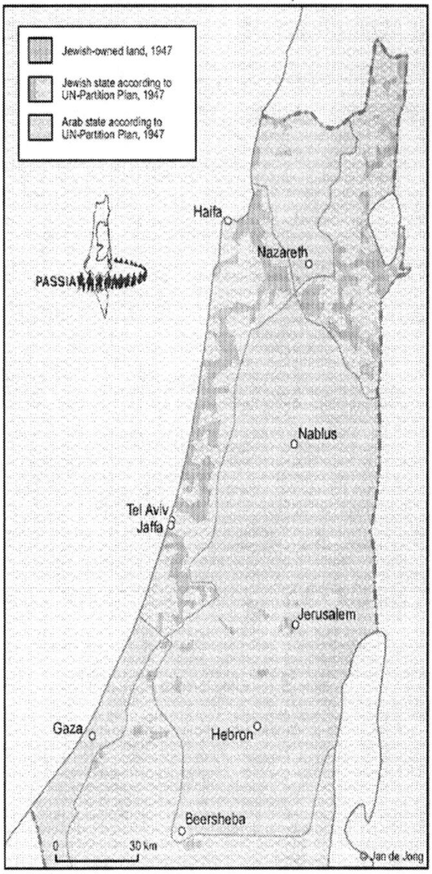

Jewish-owned land, 1947

Jewish state according to UN-Partition Plan, 1947

Arab state according to UN-Partition Plan, 1947

Haifa

Nazareth

PASSIA

Nablus

Tel Aviv
Jaffa

Jerusalem

Gaza

Hebron

Beersheba

0   30 km   © Jan de Jong

Palestinian Villages Depopulated in 1948 and 1967, and Razed by Israel

Jewish-owned land, 1947

State of Israel according to the Armistice Agreement, 1949

Palestinian villages depopulated in 1948 and 1967 and razed by Israel

The West Bank and Gaza Strip

Haifa

Nazareth

PASSIA

Nablus

Tel Aviv
Jaffa

Jerusalem

Gaza

Hebron

Beersheba

0   30 km   © Jan de Jong

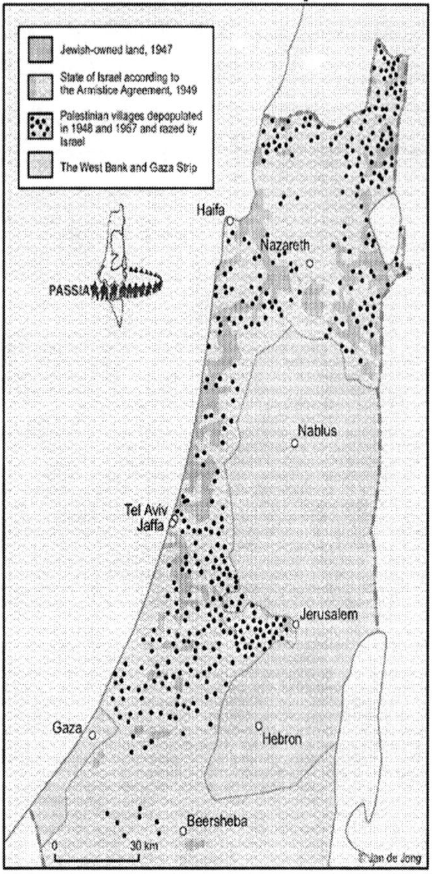

Source: Palestinian Academic Society for the Study of International Affairs (PASSIA), Jerusalem. Reprinted with permission of PASSIA.

My father joined the Jabliyah Defence Guard and took part in the skirmishes on the outskirts of town. My mother was very supportive and prayed for father's safe return. Some afternoons after school I took my father's British made rifle and went to visit school friends in the area of Tel el Rish where Arab snipers had built bunkers with sand bags not far from a Jewish settlement. Originally this was named Tell el Rous (The hill of heads) referring to the massacres committed by Napoleon's troops in Jaffa where thousands of corpses were laid on top of each other to form a hill in the outskirts of the city. We used to shoot out of the bunkers at the settlement. Yemeni volunteers, who worked in Jaffa before the fighting began, carried arms and participated in defending the city. One of them, Qassem, was in charge of defending one of the bunkers. One night a bullet hit him in his leg and he was taken to the local hospital near our house. Dr. Said Dajani who headed the hospital treated him. My father and I went to visit Qassem and took a bunch of bananas for him.

Taher (left), Qassem (middle), and school friends

At that time I was also full of mischief including taking a pistol to school, shooting a sub-machine-gun from the window towards the sea when only my grandmother was at home, and going on the roof where no one could see me and shooting a clip of bullets. During this period weapons were readily available in the black market at a high price. One day I experimented with bullets by removing the head of one, stuffing match heads over the gun powder, placing the head back on, tying a long string on both sides in the form of a sling and hurling the bullet against the wall of our house. The result was an explosion. The next time I did that the bullet exploded in my hand as I was placing the head of the bullet back on top of the gunpowder. My left thumb was split open and my father took me downtown to the pharmacy of our relative and neighbor Rachid Dajani where I was treated for the wound.

The Dajani family was very prominent in the town. Opposite the pharmacy on Iskandar Awad Street, a commercial hub, Dr. Said Dajani had a medical clinic, Dr. Jawad Abu-Rabah Dajani, had a dental clinic, Rachid Dajani had a pharmacy, Aziz Dawoodi Dajani and Shafiq Dajani had law offices, and Hassan Kholki Dajani owned a textile and clothing store. The name of Hassan was mentioned to me in 1998 by a former ambassador of Israel in the United States who was a participant at a seminar on Palestine in Washington. During his presentation, I asked the ambassador to elaborate on one of the points that came up in the discussion. When he heard my name he told me that his father used to buy textiles from Hassan Kholki on credit and sell the merchandise retail in Tel Aviv. He added that his father was very happy with the arrangement and grateful for Hassan's help. A short distance from Iskandar Awad Street lay Nuzha Street where the Dajani Hospital, founded in 1933 by Dr. Fouad Dajani, was located. Dr. Fouad, who had studied in Britain, died young and a relative, Dr. Zuhdi Dajani, took over the management of the hospital. Both Fouad and Zuhdi, together with Aziz were born in Jerusalem but made Jaffa their home.

In late April 1948 when I was 14 years old, the National Committee of the city of Jaffa advised the citizens that it was no longer safe to stay. A member of the committee was Zafer Dajani, a fourth cousin of my father and a successful businessman. The skirmishes on the outskirts of the city, which lasted several months, had then become full-blown battles, with the Jewish side having a decisive advantage because of better training, arms, and equipment. On April 9, Jewish armed militias attacked the village of Deir Yassin near Jerusalem and conducted a whole scale massacre of the villagers, including women, children and the elderly. Women were raped and bodies were looted. In all more than two hundred fifty were slaughtered. The news caused panic and a collapse of morale. In the same week Abdel-Kader al-Husseini, a popular Palestinian commander, was killed during the battle of Castal near Jerusalem, which made Palestinians feel unprotected against the Jews.[5]

Zionist leaders believed that conquering Jaffa, the cultural and commercial center of Palestine, would deal a major blow to the morale of Palestinian resistance forces, especially as Jaffa under the United Nations Partition Plan was to be part of a future Palestinian state. On April 24, 1948, my father came home late in the afternoon to tell us that Jewish fighters had encircled the city and mortars were falling on the northern part. With few arms and ammunition at our disposal, we stood no chance of protecting ourselves and we had to leave in a few hours by sea to Lebanon. This meant that only essential clothing had to be packed and taken to our fishing trawler at the harbor where the co-owner's family would be leaving at the same time. I cried and shouted, "no I am not leaving" and ran out of the house. My father ran after me and said if we were to stay the men would end up in concentration camps or be killed and the women would be raped. He then asked: Do you want your mother and sisters to be in harm's way? The question and its connotations put an end to my resistance. We left in our fishing trawler, which my father co-owned with Abu Abed Ishkuntana, in confusion, anger, and fear. We became Palestinian refugees with no valid passports, little money, and no jobs. Jaffa fell soon after following major battles where Haganah and Irgun fighters gained the upper hand. Although Jaffa surrendered without conditions and was declared an open city, the Jews did not abide by the provisions of the agreement. They plundered the city, burglarized homes and killed many civilians. Those who remained were pushed into Ajami quarter, which was encircled with wire fences.[6] My father was right when he said at the time of our exodus that if we were to stay we would be killed or end-up in concentration camps. At that time our beautiful cosmopolitan city (the Bride of the Sea and the City of Oranges), had a population of about 100,000, a thriving export sector, budding light industries, trading houses, sports clubs, and newspapers with wide circulation in Palestine. The Near East Arabic Broadcasting Station, which was established by the British Government, was located in Jaffa, and I remember a group of our neighborhood children rehearsing songs taught to them by Mr. Ansari, a schoolteacher, for a regular program of children songs. Halim al Roumi, a famous singer who also lived in our neighborhood, recorded hit songs at the station, and well-known Egyptian religious chanters contributed to the station's programs. After the end of the British Mandate in Palestine the station moved to Cyprus.

At the time of our departure Fatima came to say goodbye. She asked my mother to take Bashira, who was about five years old, with us. My mother said by all means. Fatima left for Gaza with her husband who later fell ill and died. Fatima went to Port Said, Egypt as a refugee. There she found a job as nanny with an English family. After that she married Mahmoud Dabbik, who at the time was working for an Egyptian contractor. He happened to be a classmate in my elementary school in Jaffa. After the British withdrew from the Suez Canal area, Mahmoud and Fatima settled in Cairo, Egypt.

2

Latakia

My family sailed out in the night with little food or money, a few suitcases, two hand grenades and a pistol. We had wrapped our rifle, submachine gun and twenty bullets in rubber tubes and buried them in the backyard of the house with the hope that we would retrieve them later. So many precious things were left behind, precious in terms of sentimental rather than material value. In particular most of the family photos that my brother Mahmoud had put aside in his desk drawer, ready to take with him, were forgotten at the last minute. Luckily my mother and aunt had a few pictures in their handbags. My grandfather's collection of Arabic literature, Islamic legal books and court cases were left behind.

The fishing trawler was rather crowded with our family sharing the space with the Ishkuntana family, the co-owners of the boat. Fortunately, the sea was calm and the weather good so we managed. I could see the lights of Jaffa dying behind me, and the dreams of my youth shattered and scattered in the air. Our home and the land we loved were lost to us. We were afraid of being intercepted on the sea by the Zionist Jews but luckily we had no incidents and arrived in Tyre, Lebanon in the morning. Immigration officers were standing in the port. We presented them with the documents that had been issued by the National Committee of Jaffa, identifying us as Palestinians and requesting the authorities in the host countries to give us all possible assistance. Luckily we were admitted as temporary visitors without much delay. We took a taxi and drove to al Ghaziyah, a nearby village, where my Aunt Adiba's family had earlier rented a house from a Lebanese friend. We stayed with them until we found a place to rent. A few relatives and their families followed us to al-

Ghaziyah and by the middle of June it became clear that our stay outside Palestine was going to be longer than expected.

My father and his partner agreed to send the fishing trawler with its Syrian captain Abu Abdel Latif, who worked for us in Jaffa, to Latakia, Syria where it could be put to work and provide for our livelihood. We followed on a freight train to Aleppo, Syria and spent the night sitting and sleeping on the floor of an empty car. The authorities in Aleppo directed us to a camp that had been set up for Palestinian refugees. It was a hot sweltering day and the camp seemed unbearable. We were free to find our own accommodation in town or anywhere in Syria. We hired a truck to take us with our luggage to Latakia, Syria, on the Mediterranean where we accidentally met in the city square the roving traveling Syrian Mutahher (circumcision surgeon) who had operated on us in Jaffa. He took us to his home where we spent a few nights, and he offered to rent part of the house to us. We needed a larger place, and moved to an apartment in a new building not far from the center of town. It was wonderful to see a friendly face and to be offered a helping hand.

During the early days of the summer we followed anxiously the news of the battles in Palestine between the Arab and Jewish armed forces. On May 15, 1948, following the departure of the British troops from Palestine, the neighboring Arab States sent their armies into Palestine in order to support the Palestinian paramilitary, which had about 7,000 poorly equipped troops. The Arab combat forces proved to be no match for the larger and better equipped Jewish forces. Whereas the Arabs' weapons supply suffered from the British embargo on shipments, Israel's Communist Party was able to get a large shipment of heavy arms from Czechoslovakia and the Soviet Union.[7] The result was an inevitable Arab defeat. It was such a humiliating blow for every one of us. Seventy eight percent of the historic homeland of the Palestinians was lost. By early 1949, Israel had occupied the Negev desert up to the Egypt-Palestine line except for the Gaza Strip, which was left in the administrative control of Egypt. The west Bank, which was assigned to the Arab State under the Partition Plan, was taken by Jordan and was annexed in 1950. Estimates by the United Nations of the number of Palestinian refugees displaced in 1948 totaled

957,000. Of this population, approximately one-third fled to the West Bank, another third to the Gaza Strip, and the remainder to Jordan, Syria, Lebanon or farther afield.[8] On December 11, 1948, UN General Assembly Resolution 194 asserted that refugees wishing to return to their homes and live in peace should be allowed to do so.[9] To this day my family has not been allowed to return to Palestine, nor have any other Palestinian refugees.

During the first few months in Latakia my father's financial position became critical. He sold the handgun he brought with him from Jaffa to the grocer across the street from the apartment. For a few days we ate mainly bread and olive oil sparkled with zaatar (dried oregano and thyme, similar to Italian seasoning). Soon our captain found a fishing crew to man the boat. The daily catch was at first encouraging and the money flowing in exceeded the cost of the operation. However, after about a year, the crank of the German-made Deutz engine developed a crack that could not be fixed and no replacement was available. The boat was taken to the Island of Arwad, the home of captain Abu-Abdellatif, off the shores of Tartus and put up for sale. While in Libya we received a message that the boat could not be sold and was abandoned.

We moved to a lower rent apartment and for a while we had to make do with the bare necessities until my brother Mahmoud, who had graduated from secondary school with a matriculation certificate, found a teaching position at Terre Santa School in Latakia. The principal, a Catholic priest by the name of Father Salem, hailed from Palestine. The faculty and the student body were both Muslim and Christian. They got along very well. Mahmoud proved to be an excellent teacher of mathematics and soon had more demand for private lessons than he could meet. He was able to cover a significant part of the family budget. My father also found a job as a clerk at Latakia's government mashtal (agricultural experimental station and nursery) where he had a lot of spare time to write poetry and dwell on the Nakba (catastrophe) of Palestine. My uncle found a clerical position with a lawyer. The family income was augmented by monthly food allowances from UNRWA (United Nations Relief and Work Agency). These included dried milk, sugar, rice, vegetable oil, and cod liver oil. The latter I swallowed and quickly shoved a slice of lemon in my mouth to overcome the ghastly taste. This was the worst financial crisis we were to go through.

My paternal grandmother Fatima died in early 1949 after a long illness. Her departure was hard on us being away from Jaffa and our house where she used to sit by the window of her room overlooking the sea, reading the Qur'an and praying. We used to congregate around the coal brazier in the winter to hear her tell stories before we went to bed. She smoked and I would go to her asking for a puff, she would refuse, but I would not take no for an answer until she let me have a little puff. At times I annoyed her by touching her back while she was doing her prayers. Whenever I fell ill I went to her. She would place her hand on my forehead and recite verses from the Qur'an. She left behind a legacy of love, knowledge and strong family ties.

My brother Sidqi and I enrolled in Latakia governmental secondary school. Although I was a year ahead of Sidqi in Palestine, we were placed in the same class (4th secondary) because the school system in Syria required those going to the 5th secondary grade to have passed a state-wide examination called Breve'. I did not mind being in the same class with my younger brother. I was not a good student, and spent a lot of time with friends after school. When I studied my mind wandered off and I found it difficult to concentrate. I loved to listen to Arabic music and sing. I was fond of seeing American movies. At night after the movies I would stand in front of the mirror donning a hat similar to that of Humphrey Bogart's and try to imitate the film stars by changing facial and eye expressions. In class I used to distract Sidqi by drawing pictures of famous movie actors like Tyron Power and passing them for his comments. At the end of the school year we sat for the daunting examination. Sidqi passed and I failed. The results were announced on the radio. Upon hearing Sidqi's name and not mine I ran out of the house into the darkness. What a blow to my pride even though I knew I deserved it. I walked briskly for a while and returned home after I cooled down.

My mother overwhelmed me with her love and attentiveness. Years later Sidqi told me that mother said to him, "at this stage my sympathy and attention will be given to Taher and your turn will come later." My relations with Sidqi continued to be as close as ever. We used to have long conversations about films we saw together, songs we sang and also about views relating to Islam and politics. At that time he was of the view that religion and politics are inseparable. I held the opposite view. Whenever our argument heated up he was kind enough to relent and to let me have the last word.

Taher (left) with Sidqi in Latakia

During this period Mahmoud introduced us to classical music. He used to bring home records of major composers, e.g. Beethoven, Brahms, and Rimsky-Korsakov. He also brought home contemporary and classical Arabic literature, which he shared with us.

Mahmoud suggested that I enroll at Terra Santa School where he taught. I took his advice. The teachers were good and I settled down in class. I was exempted from paying tuition because my brother was a teacher in the school. At the end of the year I passed the Breve'. I then

decided to go back to the Government school. I enrolled in the fifth secondary grade. I passed and then went up to the crucial sixth grade where at
the end of the year I had to sit for another statewide examination (the Bac-
calaureate). I passed from the first round, what a relief. I was 18 years old.
The year before Sidqi passed after the second round and went to teach elementary school at Kirdaha, the birth place of Hafez al Assad, former president of Syria, in the Alawite mountains near Latakia. Hafez al Assad was in
my Secondary School and graduated two years before I did.

Mahmoud left with Taher

We moved to a better apartment in the Tabiyat quarter, a cliff overlooking on the east a bay with a sandy shore dotted with sand dunes and
the Al-Kabir River. Beyond that stood the Alawite Mountains that were
covered in snow in the winter and provided breathtaking views of the sun
rise. On the west side lay the city, which had a population of about fifty
thousand, half Moslem and half Christian. One of the famous Arab poets

(Abu al Ala' al Maarrie) said in one of his poems "The great sounds in Latakia are shared between Ahmad (another name for the prophet Mohammad) and Christ. One rings a bell and the other from a minaret calls for prayers."

Latakia, being farther north on the eastern Mediterranean coast near Turkey, was much colder in the winter than Jaffa. The cold wind blowing from the Alawite Mountains in the east and Jabal al Aqra'a (Bald Mountain) in the north, both of which were capped with snow, caused us to wear layers of clothes and woolen gloves walking to the school. My sisters went to an elementary school close to the apartment and became friends with our neighbors' children.

Latakia had two parts, the old city and the new city. The old part had narrow alleys, charming homes and a bazaar. The new part, most of which was built during the French mandate, stretched towards the coast with modern homes, coffee houses and a cornice (promenade). Off the cornice stood the Casino Hotel overlooking the water. Teenage students, including myself, as well as teachers used to walk the length of the cornice several times in the afternoons, weather permitting. This provided an on-the-town outing and a place to meet school friends.

Among Mahmoud's private students was pretty and dashing Ninon. Two times Mahmoud asked me to be a watchman while he was teaching Ninon lest Ninon's father arrived at the house unexpectedly. The two young people fell in love and became engaged before Mahmoud left for the United States to study. Our two families visited each other and I remember Ninon's parents, brother and sister arriving in their private car at our apartment for lunch. Ninon's father, Mihrez Sakr was a sophisticated man who got his college education in Montpellier, France where he met and married Juliet Cavallier. He told us that while a student he got to know one of my father's cousins, Thafer Dajani, who was in the same college. What a small world? Judge Abdelrahman Dajani, who headed the Shari'a Court in Latakia, attended Mahmoud's engagement ceremony. After the exodus from Jaffa, Abdelrahman and his wife Hasiba went to Syria where he was appointed a judge in Kamishli, on the Euphrates River in northeastern Syria near the Turkish and Iraqi borders. It was a source of pride for our family to have him transfer to Latakia.

I loved to swim in the bay near our apartment and walk alone or with friends towards the river. I loved to sing in that empty space while walking around the sand dunes, which dotted the area.

Taher standing third from left with school friends at Latakia harbor

I started to smoke cigarettes regularly, although the first time I smoked was in Jaffa with brother Mahmoud and my first cousins Ata and Hamed. Latakia was famous for its tobacco and I used to roll my own cigarettes. After several admonitions and punishments my father gave up on me, and I began to smoke in front of him at age sixteen. Of course, he was a smoker and so were my Uncle Ishaq and my grandmother. My brother Mahmoud also smoked and he could afford to buy imported English cigarettes much to my envy, but he was kind enough to let me borrow one or two once in a while.

I earned my first paycheck at age nineteen working for two weeks in the summer at a factory that was run by Ninon's father. The factory crushed olive pits and the product (Arjoun) was used as an energy source in bakery ovens and for heating. My job was to weigh the product before it was loaded onto trucks. With the money I earned I bought an inexpensive violin and started to take lessons. My teacher was an old Greek gentleman with a white curly moustache. His son, who worked for a shipping firm at the port, played the instrument very well. After every lesson the maestro offered me a home made aperitif, with a little alcohol content, which he was fond of drinking. I learned the notes and how to hold the violin and the bow and practiced faithfully what I learned.

I applied for a teaching job and was offered one in Kamishli in northeast Syria. At the same time my father started to teach English, which he learned in secondary school in Palestine and at the American University of Beirut, Lebanon, in a town about 100 miles south of Latakia. He came home over the weekends. In the fall of 1952, I went to study law at the University of Syria in Damascus following the steps of brother Mahmoud who also enrolled at the same university to study chemistry.

Law students were required to be in attendance a minimum of one month as external students while science students were required to be there the full school year. Tuition was free. Mahmoud spent only two months in Damascus. He met a fellow student, Fathi Said, from secondary school in Jaffa who told him that he had applied to the University of Texas in Austin and received a letter of admission, and that he planned to travel there as soon as he received a visa from the United States Embassy. Mahmoud decided to do the same because of the prestige attached to obtaining education in America. It did not take long for Mahmoud to get admission and as soon as he and his friend got the visas they flew to Austin, Texas. Each had enough money to finance the first semester, and hoped to be able to work to cover tuition and living expenses. After one semester in Austin, Mahmoud and his friend Fathi moved to Chicago where they hoped it would be easier to find work while studying in the big city.

I stayed in Damascus the minimum time required for attendance by an external student. Luckily my living expenses were covered by a grant to the

University from UNRWA for Palestinian students. However, this was not automatic and the Administrator said I did not qualify because I was an external student. So I went to the office of the President of the University and spoke to his secretary, who seemed to dislike the Administrator. He said the President had a visitor with him but you go right ahead. I explained to the President (Dr. Jabri), who came from the same family as my mother, my dire need for the grant and told him I had borrowed money to cover the expenses of my stay in Damascus. He wrote a note to the Administrator asking him to write an order to pay. I received the equivalent of US $400 at current 2007 U.S. prices. It was the largest sum I had ever put my hand on. I had very little money in Damascus and by the middle of the month I had to borrow from a friend, Fayez Kilani, who owned a fancy women's shoe store, whom I met through Mahmoud and Ninon. Fayez was in love with one of Ninon's friends, who was a customer. Well-to-do Latakians traveled to Damascus or Beirut for shopping. I repaid Fayez his money and felt happy to have spare cash.

The university campus was walking distance from the building where I lived. Several of my friends from secondary school went to the same college and we ate lunch together at the cafeteria, which offered good food at a reasonable cost. After lunch I used to go to one of the rooms in the building where a group of musicians practiced. I was impressed with their expertise on the cello and the violin. They played old Arabic tunes that stirred my passion for the violin.

My friends and I did a lot of partying in the apartment and I did not study hard enough; I failed the course on Islamic Law, which I was supposed to repeat in the second round of examinations in the summer. This did not materialize as my father signed up for a job with the Libyan American Technical Assistance Service (LATAS) to work as an expert in agricultural extension in al Marj near Benghazi, Libya, in the Green Mountain area. This was a major turning point for the family as my father's teaching job one hundred miles from Latakia caused him to live away from the family during working days. My brother Sidqi who had been teaching for one year in Kirdaha was offered a position at a higher salary in Ariha near Aleppo. My uncle who was visiting that town with some friends, heard about an opening in the junior secondary school there, and he arranged the interview. Sidqi moved to Ariha with our uncle and aunt. Mahmoud went to study in the United States and the rest of the family, including myself, joined my father in Libya.

During the four years we spent in Syria, there were three coup d'etats. In April 1949, on the heels of the defeat of Syrian and other Arab forces by Israel, the army chief Hosni al Zaim toppled the democratically elected government of Shukri al Kuwatli. This bloodless military coup was the first in Syria and the Arab world. Zaim was soon overthrown by a coup waged by Colonel Sami al Hinnawi who restored Syria's parliamentary system. A new government headed by a veteran nationalist, Hashem Atassi, was formed and Hinnawi became chief of staff of the Syrian Army. The Government did not survive long because Atassi wanted to create a union with the Hashemite Kingdom of Iraq, a move that was opposed by Colonel Adib Shishekli and other officers.

In December 1949, Shishekli launched the third coup and arrested Hinnawi to suppress the Hashemite influence in Syria, but he kept Attasi at his post. In the following two years the civilian government tried to stabilize the situation, but without a strong leader it was unable to maintain authority. In 1951, Shishekli abolished all political parties and tried to fill the vacuum by creating his own party, which was boycotted by the civilian political elite. He banished the Ba'ath party leaders to Lebanon and also persecuted other parties, including the Communist Party and the Muslim Brotherhood. He frequently clashed with the Druze minority and bombarded their province accusing them of wanting to topple his regime using funds from Jordan.

His foreign policy did not please the United Kingdom or the United States. At the beginning the United Kingdom had courted Shishekli, hoping that he would join the Baghdad Pact, which was allied with the West against the Soviet Union. He was not in favor of the Pact because the majority of the Syrian people were against it. I remember the demonstrations against the Baghdad Pact that took place while I was at the University of Syria. One student stood up and said if the Government were to join the Pact, blood would run in the streets so much as to cover one's legs up to one's knees. The feeling was strong against the West because of the recent colonial history in the region.

The United States was rumored to have offered Shishekli large sums of money to settle Palestinian refugees in Syria and to give them citizenship. He did not take the offer, mainly because he believed the Arabs should liberate Palestine and send the refugees back home.

Growing domestic discontent eventually led to the ousting of Shishekli in 1954. The plotters included members of the Communist and Ba'ath parties and disgruntled Druze officers. He fled to Lebanon and then to Brazil, where a Syrian Druze who was seeking revenge for the bombardment of Jabal Druze assassinated him.[10]

In the following years other coup d'etats took place in neighboring Arab countries. In 1952, Gamal Abdel Nasser and a group of military officers launched a successful coup in Egypt that deposed King Farouk. The new revolutionary regime introduced major reorientation in economic policy, including agrarian reform, and inspired anti-colonial and Pan-Arab nationalist policies in the region.

In 1958, a group of political and military leaders in Syria led by then President Kuwatli proposed a merger with Egypt to President Nasser who welcomed the proposal, and both signed the pact creating the United Arab Republic following a referendum conducted in the two countries. However, the union collapsed in 1961 after a coup d'etat in Syria brought a secessionist group to power. The separation was deeply contested in Syria and a bitter struggle ensued until the Ba'ath Party, Nasserites and other pro-union elements took power in 1963. Three years later the Ba'ath launched a coup within the regime and cleared out the other parties from the government. Hafez al Assad, who was in my secondary school in Latakia, became Minister of Defense and in 1971 he became the President of Syria. Assad's rule stabilized and strengthened the power of the central government after decades of coups and counter coups. Upon his death in 2000 his son Bashar was elected president.[11]

Subhia Dajani, 1956

Tayeb Dajani, 1952

My Mother with Khawla (left), Bashira, and Salwa

3

Tripoli

On the way to Libya the family stopped in Beirut for a few days, which gave us a chance to see my Aunt Adiba and her family who had moved from Ghaziya to Beirut because of the children's education. We also visited several Dajanis who had made Beirut their temporary home. We flew out of Beirut to Benghazi in July 1953. The chartered flight that was provided for us by LATAS was a small turbo prop. The trip took about four hours and was very bumpy. My mother and sisters felt sick and could not eat any lunch on the plane.

We spent one night in Benghazi in one of the rest houses rented by LATAS and then drove to Al Marj in Jabal al-Akhdar (Green Mountain), which during the Italian colonization of Libya (1911–1945) witnessed major battles between the Libyan resistance movement, led by Omar al Mukhtar, and the Italian military forces. We drove up a winding road through scenic hills to our destination. My father whom we had not seen for a few months was waiting for us and we were happy to be together again. We stayed in his bachelor's apartment for a few days and then moved to a house that my dad rented from the municipality.

Al Marj was a small agricultural town with a few paved roads, one elementary school and one doctor from the World Health Organization. LATAS had a technical assistance station in the town to help farmers improve their production techniques. My father worked as an assistant to the American head of the station and he seemed to enjoy his job. Social life was limited. There were a few Palestinians working for the provincial government and the United Nations. My mother still had a large family to take care of with my Father, Salwa, Khawla, Bashira, and myself at home.

The house we moved into was a three-bedroom rambler with a kitchen and a bathroom. A high wall encircled the paved front yard, and the back yard was bare except for one tree. Italian colonists had built the house. Our neighbors were the Mayor of the town who belonged to one of the largest tribes (Obeidat) and Sayed al Siddik al Senusi, a relative of King Idris who ruled over the Kingdom of Libya after the Allies defeated Italy in the Second World War. Siddik's son Sharif, about my age, was sociable and loved to play the piano and sing. We became friends.

Sayed Siddik employed a young Palestinian law graduate, Nayef Farris, to manage his farm. He gave him an office and living quarters. I got to know Nayef and used to go to his office frequently to learn to type English touch method. It was not easy at the beginning but I eventually learned to type at a speed of about twenty words a minute. At that time my violin gave me a lot of pleasure until it broke when I sat on it by mistake. After several months a friend of my father brought me a violin from Rome for the equivalent of fifty dollars. I still have that violin today.

My father was on the lookout for a job for me as my studies were on hold. He was told there was a vacancy at a nearby agricultural training school that was being administered by LATAS. The position was for teaching Arabic and religion. I had an interview with the principal of the school (Mr. Johnson) who was a king-sized Texan in his sixties. I was hired and lived on campus, about one hour's drive from home. I worked hard preparing for Arabic grammar classes and did well as a teacher. However, the job proved to be temporary as the department of education in Benghazi decided to replace me with an Egyptian university graduate who would be financed by the Government of Egypt. Earlier two Egyptian graduates in agriculture had come to teach at the school.

My brother Sidqi came to visit us in the summer. He flew to Cairo from Damascus and then took a bus to Alexandria and all the way to Benghazi. He arrived at the house in al Marj unannounced and we were thrilled and delighted. He spoke in detail about his job and his students. He spoke about his uncle and aunt who lived with him and took care of his daily house chores and food. Sidqi was endowed with an excellent memory and a knack for details and story telling. He spoke of his plans to enroll at the university in Damascus to study history while working in Ariha. We talked about the hit songs and sang together. We continued to argue, sometimes heatedly about political subjects and sometimes about who the best movie actors were in Egypt and Hollywood, and the best Arabic and English fiction writers whose novels were translated into Arabic. At that time I was nineteen years old and he was seventeen years old.

A relative of ours (Atif Azzouni) whose mother was a sister of Hamdi Dajani, the principal of our elementary school in Jaffa, came to visit. He worked for the Arab Bank in Benghazi headed by Khalil Dawoodi. I told him I was planning to study in America, had applied to universities there and had been practicing my English typing. Soon after, a message came to my father from Khalil that the Bank had a position for a typist. I went to Benghazi and was hired. Atif suggested that we look for a room to share. We found a room at the top of a house that was rented by a Turkish couple. We stayed in that room only a few days as the mosquitoes and the heat at night took their toll. We went to a pension run by an Italian woman and luckily we found a large room with two beds, which we rented. What a relief to have comfortable accommodation.

I enjoyed my work at the bank where I mostly typed letters of credit and got along well with the staff, five in all. Typing under pressure for a beginner like me was very difficult but my colleagues were very patient and understanding. One afternoon after the bank closed to the public the two cashiers, who were both Palestinian, quarreled and got into a brutal fight where staplers and hole punchers were used as weapons. I tried to separate the two but to no avail. Blood seeped from their faces with no proclaimed winner. Khalil asked me to come to his office and told me to sit there with him, which I did. At that point I felt like I was acting as his personal bodyguard. He was highly nervous and frightened. After that day Khalil and I became friends.

Benghazi was Libya's second largest city and a number of prominent Libyan families lived there. While in Benghazi I met Dawood Abed, a Palestinian who worked in the personnel department of the Federal Government. He told me about a position of clerk/translator in his office. I applied and was hired and left the bank.

In Al Marj my father had problems at work. Two of the Palestinians with the department of agriculture who were jealous of my father's position with LATAS ganged up against him and complained to their Libyan manager, who was a relative of the Senusi family (the royal family of Libya), that my father was unhelpful. The manager called my father's supervisor to his office and told him that coordination between them would be jeopardized if my father continued to work in that job. Faced with this crisis my father went to see our neighbor Sayed Siddiq Senusi and explained to him his side of the story. Sayed Siddiq, who did not think highly of his relative's judgment, summoned my father's supervisor and asked him to inform his head office in Tripoli that the allegations against my father were untrue and that the Libyans were happy with my father's services.

Soon after that my father was transferred to Tripoli much to the happiness of my mother and sisters. My mother did not have much of a social life in al Marj. Khawla and Bashira had finished the highest grade in the elementary school and no secondary education was available. Salwa had spent a whole year without schooling and felt very pleased and relieved at the prospect of continuing her education. I remained in Benghazi a few more months until the Federal Government moved to Tripoli. At that time the seat of the government rotated annually between the two cities.

I moved to Tripoli and reunited with the family in early 1954. I was so impressed by this beautiful city, with its long sandy beaches and lush farms filled with olive trees, palms, grapevines and orange groves. Its Mediterranean climate and moderate temperatures reminded me of Jaffa, except for the ghibli wind, which comes from the Sahara desert and reaches hurricane speeds in North Africa and Southern Europe. It arises from a warm, dry, tropical air mass that is pulled northward by low-pressure cells moving eastward across the Mediterranean Sea.

The ghibli, most common during the autumn and spring, may last one day or many days and it causes very dry conditions. The fine sand it carries gets in one's mouth, into one's clothes and through the tightest windows and doors. Walking becomes almost impossible as the fine grains of sand sting one's eyes and skin. Indoors everything becomes covered with a thin layer of sand. Notwithstanding the ghibli, Tripoli charmed me with its mosaic background: Phoenician, Roman, Byzantium and Islamic, and with its metropolitan Arab-Italian atmosphere. I continued to work with the Government in the same position. The family lived in a nice three-bedroom apartment. My sister Salwa enrolled in Tripoli Teachers College, as there were no secondary schools available at that time. Khawla and Bashira continued in junior high and I was able to start taking violin lessons again.

The Italian maestro, who was in his late seventies, spoke neither Arabic nor English, but we managed to communicate about the time of my lessons and the exercises to be covered. His studio was about twenty minutes walk from the apartment. At times he came to our apartment for the lessons and when he did we served him Arabic coffee and home made pastries. I practiced a lot in my spare time and enjoyed playing simplified and popular classical tunes from La Traviata and La Boheme as well as two tangos: La Comparsita and La Paloma, but my playing was in the early stages and tentative.

In the summer I went swimming at the Lido beach and got to know a few young Libyans. In my spare time I used to like walking on the cornice which stretched along the harbor or sitting in a cafe' along Istiklal street, an attractive shopping area with beautiful arcades and trees along the road where young people walked in the summer afternoons up and down the street. One café used to invite music bands from Italy that played and sang the latest hits. A local cinema also invited opera companies to perform and I took mother to see the Barber of Seville and La Boheme. There was a score of Palestinians in Tripoli at that time who mostly worked for the Government. My parents got to know and socialize with several of the families.

Government employees were provided with bus transportation to the building of the Federal Government, which for me was a fifteen-minute ride from the center of town near where we lived. At the bus stop I met Maria, an Italian typist working for the Government. She asked me to teach her Arabic. I went to her apartment and gave her several lessons but they did not last long. After that we stopped the lessons but continued to be friends. In addition, I met Pupa who also worked for the government. We enjoyed each other's company and went swimming at the Lido beach on the outskirts of town.

After a few months with the personnel department I transferred to the Ministry of Trade as a translator, a job that allowed me to substantially improve my written English. My brother Mahmoud came to visit Tripoli on his return to the States after having gone to Latakia to wed Ninon. Judge Dajani conducted the signing of the wedding contract ceremony. I enjoyed Mahmoud's company and we went sightseeing with a Palestinian friend who had a car.

I asked Mahmoud to help me apply to DePaul University in Chicago where he was studying at the time. I sent him a copy of my secondary school certificate and he went to see Father Quigley, the Dean of the college of Commerce. I got accepted. But there was a major hurdle facing me. I had no passport and my Syrian travel document had expired and had to be renewed in Damascus, as there was no embassy in Tripoli.

I asked Khalil Dawoodi, who had left the Arab Bank in Benghazi and joined the Federal Government as a senior staff member, to help me get a Libyan travel document that would allow me to travel to the United States. He went to the Prime Minister (Abdel Majid Ku'bar) and explained my situation to him. A letter was sent to the Immigration department and a travel document was issued to me by order of the Prime Minister. It really was a stroke of luck to get this document and I will always be thankful for Khalil's help.

4

Chicago

In October 1955, I flew from Tripoli to New York with an overnight stop in Paris and a stop in Greenland. My parents, sisters, Pupa and several relatives and friends came to the airport to bid me goodbye. Fred Barber, who was my father's boss at LATAS in al-Marj, and his wife were at the airport heading for a vacation in Rome. Mrs. Barber turned to me and said that life in the United States could be hard, that she at one time had to clean floors to earn pocket money and that I should be prepared to slog it out.

From New York I took a Greyhound bus to Chicago. I was thrilled to see the skyscrapers as we left Manhattan and as we approached Chicago. I felt happy to have reached my destination but worried about making a living and getting an education with a lot of unknowns in a new environment.

My brother Mahmoud arranged for me to stay with his Palestinian friends (Fathi Said, Walid Bibi and Omar Abu Gheida) who lived in a rented apartment in the north side of the city until I found my own accommodation. Mahmoud lived in a rented room on Freemont Street near DePaul University and I found a small apartment on Webster Avenue in the same neighborhood.

I arrived in Chicago with only $300 in my pocket, which I had saved. This sum translates into $2,300 at current 2007 prices. My father borrowed money from a friend to pay for my air ticket. My money was barely enough to cover one semester's expense in college. Mahmoud and I went to see Father Quigley, the Dean of the College of Commerce at DePaul, to ask for a deferral of my admission by one semester in order to improve my English. He agreed. Immediately thereafter I began to look for a job. Mahmoud and all his Palestinian friends were working their way through college and I was determined to do the same. Anyway, it was a necessity.

Through the classified section of the Chicago Tribune I found a clerical job at a furniture store and was hired by the deputy manager. When the manager showed up 3 days later he sent me a letter terminating my job because of unfamiliarity with store procedures. The letter of termination I received over the weekend had a check for $50, as my wage for the week. It was shocking and humiliating, particularly as the letter was sent to Mahmoud's address and his landlady was present when I read the letter.

My second job was also clerical at a small company that manufactured engine parts for trucks. I was to assist the accountant and answer the telephone at a salary of $50 a week. After a month the owner told me his brother had been made redundant and he needed to give him my position. Another blow but I didn't give up. My third job was at a factory that manufactured metal shades for neon lights. I worked a night shift as a laborer at $1.60 an hour ($ 12.40 at current 2007 prices). I was laid off after one month as the company decided to close the night shift.

Feeling desperate and worried about finding an office job before the semester began I borrowed a typewriter from a friend of ours and spent a week working up my speed. I then went to the State employment agency to look for a typing position. I took a test that resulted in a score of thirty-five words a minute compared to a required minimum of forty-two words. I was sent for an interview with Peter Douglas, Manager of Association Consolidators, a small freight handling company that specialized in shipping merchandise from Chicago to the south east of the country, by aggregating small shipments into one freight car for certain railroad destinations, e.g. Mobile, Alabama and Jacksonville, Florida.

The office was located at 475 East Randolph Street in downtown Chicago. It was a devil to find. I walked on Randolph going east toward the Lake but the street ended at the Prudential Building on Michigan Avenue and Lake Shore Drive. The number 475 did not exist. I went back to where I started and took a taxi but the driver ended up at the same point at Lake Shore Drive. I took another taxi and the driver found his way by going to the road network under the downtown area.

We found the office near the end of a railroad track close to Lake Michigan and a huge garbage dump. In the year 2005 I revisited the address and much to my surprise it had been converted to a small park. The garbage dump had disappeared and the land has become an extension to a thriving tourist attraction complex at the Lake, called the Chicago Pier.

The interview with Peter Douglas went well. He explained to me that my job would be to go through the bills of lading for each shipment and figure out the charges in dollar terms by multiplying the weight by the rate quoted for the shipment. Moreover, I would be responsible for bookkeeping tasks. The salary offered was $60 a week. This job would turn out to be a turning point in my life in Chicago. After working a month I telephoned Peter on the weekend and told him that I would be going to college in January and I needed to have flexible working hours. I was so apprehensive that he might tell me that this wouldn't work. Luckily he agreed that I could work after I finished my classes at around 1.00 PM and go home after I finished my jobs for the day, which would be around 7.00 PM. On Friday nights the work extended until very late in the evening and often until midnight so I ended up working full time. Although this was a demanding schedule I enjoyed it and my English started improving enormously.

The office space was rather tight, occupying an area of the loading dock. It had a furnace for heating, a window air conditioner, and 4 desks. A black board hung on one of the walls on which the foreman (Ed Underwood) who worked for the railroad recorded the names of the destination cities for which shipments were being loaded in the railway cars. The staff of Association Consolidators consisted of Peter Douglas and Paul Brennan who besides typing the manifests assisted Peter in receiving the business calls and in quoting the rates for each shipment. A seminary college student worked part time as a typist. All the laborers who carried the shipments from trucks into the railroad cars worked for the railroad company. They were mostly African Americans and Ukrainians who spoke little English and were called displaced persons (DP's), which reminded me of the Palestinian people and myself.

Peter Douglas was friendly. He came to America from England as a foster child during World War II. He was a good student and graduated from the University of Chicago with a Bachelor degree in English literature. Early on he invited me to have dinner and spend the weekend at his home where I met his wife, mother-in-law, and children. Paul Brennan also invited me to his house where I met his mother, sister and brothers; and Ed Underwood was kind enough to ask me to join him and his wife for a game of bowling. On Friday nights when we stayed late to finish the work all of the office staff had shots of whiskey to sustain them and then, during the college football season, we tried to close early, as we loved to go to a tavern in downtown to watch the game.

After Ninon's arrival in Chicago in 1956 Mahmoud and I rented a two-bedroom apartment on Clarendon Street near Belmont Ave. in the north side. The semester had just started and my first class began at 8:00 AM. I took the bus an hour earlier to get there on time. I made sandwiches for lunch, which I ate at work. As mentioned I worked from around 1:00 PM to 7:00 PM and walked back about twenty minutes to the subway on State Street and headed home. Ninon would have dinner ready and I would eat around 8:00 PM. I tried to study for two hours in a state of total exhaustion. The courses on mathematics and statistics proved dry and difficult.

Mahmoud worked in the afternoon at the laboratory of Nalco Chemical Inc. in the south side of Chicago. He arrived home from work at around 11:00 PM. On Wednesday evenings Ninon and I watched Play House 90 after dinner. Ronald Reagan introduced the show, which was invariably dramatic and exciting. A few Palestinian students lived close by and on some weekends we would socialize and sometimes go to nightclubs downtown.

Mahmoud had a 1949 Dodge, which he drove to the university in downtown Chicago and to work. I started to look for a used car. I went to a dealership and found a six-year-old Ford. I got cheated. The salesman altered the price agreed upon from $300 to $600. I signed the finance papers without noticing the changes. I was very upset and the following day I went to the owner of the dealership, a slight Jewish man, and told him I had just started college and there was no way I could meet the monthly payments. I took with me two small ornamented wooden boxes that I bought in Tripoli to use as future gifts and gave them to him. He then changed the price to $350 and I took the car. This was a hard lesson learned early in life and a second one was still to come. Now to this day I read every word of a contract very carefully and never fail to bargain, no matter what the product or service I am interested in.

I had taken a few driving lessons in Jaffa at the age of thirteen with money I got from my mother in return for clearing a blockage in the main drainage near the front door. For the lessons the teacher and I drove on the outskirts of town to Ramat Gan, a Jewish colony that was established on Palestinian land during the British mandate. It was a shock for me to see foreign people in modern homes secluded from the rest of Jaffa. A group of young Jewish boys and girls were standing at one of the intersection talking and laughing. We stopped the car and I tried to speak to one of the girls in Arabic and in beginner's English. She smiled and spoke in a language that I did not understand.

I had thought that after a few lessons with Mahmoud I would be able to pass the driving test. I flunked the parallel parking segment of the test. I told the young man who tested me that I was working my way through college and could not easily come back for another test. I passed him a $5 bill and said please help me. He did and I got my driving license, but until today I still feel uneasy for what I did, although bribery was rampant in Chicago in the 1950's.

It was so scary to start driving on the busy highways. Exiting at Belmont into Lake Shore Drive for the first time caused my hands to shake and my stomach to sink. Later, on two occasions I was stopped for traffic violations and I handed the police officers a $10 dollar bill and said I was a foreign student and asked them to help me. Both let me go. I was lucky I did not end up in jail. At that time it was no secret that the traffic police were corrupt. It took a new police chief several years later to clean up the police department in Chicago. The chief's name was Captain Wilson hired from the Los Angeles police department. I started to drive to college and found parking near the freight office of the railroad under Michigan Ave., a short walking distance from the office and the university.

In my second semester I had an infection under my arm that caused me severe pain and discomfort. I went to Grant Hospital for surgery and stayed there for a week. I did not have insurance and covered the cost amounting to $250 by paying monthly installments. Peter Douglas came to visit me in the hospital and gave me my week's pay. I believe that my treating physician Dr. Vulgaris, Mahmoud's family doctor, and the lady surgeon, whose name I cannot recall, must have reduced their fees because I was a student. Dr. Vulgaris jokingly told the nurses who cared for me to be careful of Oriental boys. Later, I dated one of the nurses several times. My first priority after I left the hospital was to buy medical insurance. I contacted Blue Cross Blue Shield and bought a policy, which I kept during the rest of my stay in the United States

I did not do well in my second semester mainly because of the mathematics and statistics courses, which were hard for me. I was put on probation. This was a wake up call that prompted me to cut back on going out to nightclubs during weekends and do more studying.

Meanwhile, Ninon became pregnant and she gave birth to Samir in April 1957 and we were all very thrilled with the cute baby. On a few occasions I babysat Samir when Mahmoud and Ninon went out on weekends to visit friends. After a few months Mahmoud found an apartment near Lawrence Ave., and I found an efficiency apartment nearby. In 1958 Mahmoud and Ninon had a beautiful baby daughter whom they named Aida.

I slugged it out one semester after another carrying twelve credit hours a semester and taking six credit hours every summer. In my sophomore year I met Ellen Herhold, who lived nearby. I invited her to the Chicago annual fair and we became friends.

I had sold my old car as junk and bought a more recent Ford model, black with a white top. As happened before, I had a bad experience with the small car dealership. After completing the paper work and putting a down payment I drove the car home. In the evening I went over the finance papers that I signed. Much to my surprise I found the price was altered and my monthly payments were much higher than agreed upon verbally. The next day I told my boss the story and said that the dealer was likely to call him to verify the status of my employment and salary for the purpose of financing the car. I asked him to tell the dealer that I only worked part time and my salary was much below the level mentioned in the papers. As expected, the dealer called that morning and was told the bad news. In the afternoon I went to the dealer. His pretty young wife was standing with him carrying a baby. I told her about what happened and asked that the paper work be altered to show the price and the monthly payments I had originally agreed upon. Looking at the dealer angrily I shouted at him and asked: "Where is your conscience?" He went into his little office and he changed the paper work to my satisfaction.

Taher at the wheel of his Ford

In Chicago, 1960

During my student years in Chicago I closely followed the news of the Middle East. In 1956 Egyptian President Gamal Abdel Nasser nationalized the Suez Canal following the decision by the United States and the United Kingdom not to finance the construction of the Aswan Dam, as they had promised. This was a reaction to the growing ties between Egypt and the Soviet Union and Czechoslovakia. The United Kingdom and France, who owned the largest shares of the Suez Canal Company, allying with Israel, secretly prepared for military action to regain control of the Canal, and to depose President Nasser. On October 29, 1956, Israeli brigades invaded Egypt and British and French forces supported the invasion. However, growing opposition in the United Nations and Soviet threats to intervene put an end to the occupation. Israel had occupied Gaza during the invasion and dragged its feet from withdrawing but President Eisenhower pressured Israel to withdraw. Nasser emerged as the victor and liberator. He became the most popular nationalist figure in the Arab countries. The Arab students in Chicago, including myself, were thrilled at finally having a strong man who could eventually unite the Arab countries and liberate Palestine.[12] At the university I participated in a panel discussion organized by a student club about the background of the Palestinian refugee problem. As I write this, more than fifty years have gone by and we are no closer to peace, Arab unity, or getting back our lost land.

My life in large part revolved around my studies and work. I wrote regularly to my parents in Tripoli and to brother Sidqi who was studying history as a nonresident student at the University of Syria in Damascus. He was still living with Uncle Ishak and Aunt Fakhriya.

One morning while driving on Lake Shore Drive on my way to college a taxi hit me from behind. The traffic came to a halt in the left lane where I was driving. The traffic police came and gave the taxi driver a violation ticket. I called Dr. Vulgaris and told him about the accident and that my neck was sore. He asked me to stay home until I had talked to a lawyer friend of his. The lawyer came to see me at home that evening wearing his expensive suit and driving his fancy Cadillac. The next day he sent me to the hospital to make sure I was not injured and to have massage on my neck. After three days in the hospital I checked out. A suit was filed and a settlement with the taxi insurance company was reached two years later just before I returned to Tripoli. One third of the settlement, after doctors' fees and other expenses, went to the lawyer and I collected $350, equivalent to about $2,400 at current 2007 prices.

Three years after I joined Association Consolidators, Peter Douglas left his family and quit his job. For a while no one knew his whereabouts. Arthur Flanagan, who was hired by Peter upon Paul's joining the Fire Department, took over as Manager. Don Golminas was hired to fill Arthur's position. Later on Peter returned to his family and took a job with Time Magazine and then with Chase Manhattan Bank in London. His family moved to England with him. I have kept in touch with Peter and his family over the years.

Arthur was a good man and we got along well. My salary continued to increase every year reaching $120 a week, equivalent to about $50,000 a year at current prices. Arthur came to DePaul one evening to hear me speak about the expulsion of the Palestinians from their land by Israel in a panel organized by a students' club.

I graduated with a Bachelor's of Science in Commerce with a major in finance in 1959, and with a Master's in Business Administration (Finance) in 1961. Mahmoud, Ellen and Arthur Flanagan came to my graduation ceremonies.

FEB 1960

Taher at graduation with brother Mahmoud

I was lucky to get admission to graduate school because my grades were average. What made the difference was the fact that after I had finished the course requirements for the Bachelor's degree and before the official graduation I took two graduate courses as a special student and earned A's. The evening classes in graduate school suited me very well as I got the morning hours to study and do research in the library for the term papers that were assigned. My grades improved and my grade point average at graduation was B+. My paper on central banking in the United Arab Republic and Libya received an A. Ellen was kind enough to type it for me. Of course I continued to work in the afternoons until I was ready to go home.

In April 1961, after close to six years since my arrival in Chicago, I traveled home on the Queen Elizabeth from New York to Southampton. In New York I went to the Copa Cabana nightclub where Frank Sinatra was performing. While in Chicago I once went to the club Chez Paris to hear Nat King Cole sing. The next day I boarded the ship and sailed off to a long awaited reunion with my family whom I had not seen for almost six years.

Mahmoud had suggested the name of a travel agent that he worked with for his trip to Latakia, and the agent prepared a detailed itinerary for all my stops on the way to Tripoli at the lowest possible cost. On the ship I shared a windowless six-bunker room with others whom I hardly saw except late in the morning. I enjoyed the fabulous shows on the ship in the company of an older woman and a young one who were seated at the same table at dinner in the restaurant.

After arrival in Southampton I took the train to London where I spent a few days in the company of a young Indian doctor who also was on the ship. He had studied in England and said he would show me around. We found a bed and breakfast accommodation, which had the bare minimum of comfort. It was still rather cold and we had to feed the heater in the room with coins and the same for hot water in the bathroom. I found touring London very interesting. I went to the City where the Bank of England and the Stock Exchange are located; I visited the British Library, the National Gallery of Art, St. Paul's Cathedral, the Houses of Parliament, and the Tower of London. I also took a double decker bus all the way to its end run and back in order to see the residential areas.

After four days in London, I took the ferry from Dover to Calais, France, then the train to Nice, and the bus to Monte Carlo where we stopped for a break. I went to one of the famous casinos nearby and played the slot machines. The bus continued the journey to the Italian Riviera and to Naples. I spent two days sight seeing, and visited the Isle of Capri. Then came the last leg of my trip. I boarded a passenger ship (the Tunisia) to Tripoli. The ship crossed the sea to Tripoli regularly from Naples. It was not crowded and I was the only person in the cabin. I was invited to eat dinner at the Captain's table. The Mediterranean was calm and the sailing smooth in contrast to the voyage across the Atlantic where for two days out of five we went through a storm and the Queen constantly rocked so hard that the dining tables had to be anchored to the floor. The whole trip from New York to Tripoli cost me around $500 in those days, equivalent to a month's pay. It was a wonderful experience and worth every penny.

5

Back to Tripoli

At the port my parents and brother Sidqi were waiting to see me after almost 6 years. It was an emotional and happy reunion. We drove in my father's old Renault and headed to the apartment. Nothing had changed. The neighbors, the grocery store, and the furniture were familiar. My sisters Khawla and Bashira were there and I was thrilled to see them. My sister Salwa was in Syria finishing secondary school. She lived with Sidqi who had moved to Damascus in 1957 to take up a teaching job at Haifa Secondary School, which was financed by UNRWA, and to continue his college education. It was lucky for Salwa and Sidqi that Uncle Ishaq and Aunt Fakhria were there to take care of them. Later, our uncle was stricken by cancer and passed away in his late fifties.

After his graduation with a Bachelor's degree in history Sidqi went to Libya to take a position as a teacher in a school near Tripoli. He brought Aunt Fakhria with him. Salwa moved in with my mother's brother Ali and his family who had earlier moved to Damascus from Egypt where they emigrated after leaving Jaffa. A year later Sidqi transferred to Teachers College in Tripoli, which cut down on the time he spent commuting to school.

Sidqi had announced he was ready for marriage and at the suggestion of mother he traveled to Beirut to visit Kamel Dajani and meet his daughter Sana. Salwa went with him. He asked for Sana's hand in marriage and it was agreed that she would follow him to Tripoli where the wedding would take place. Sidqi took an apartment near my parents' and the wedding was held in 1960 as planned. I believe Sidqi and Sana only met this one time before marriage. Nowadays there are phone calls and e-mails after the initial meeting but much the same system prevails.

After a few days in Tripoli I began to look for a job. I went to the Arab Bank to follow up on an application I sent from Chicago and I was told that the head office had contacted them and they wanted me to go to Amman. I applied to two oil companies but was told I was over qualified for the job openings. Sidqi tried to connect me with friends at the department of finance, Tripolitania provincial government, but no jobs were available. I had written to the Bank of Libya seeking a job but had not received a response by the time I left Chicago, although the Bank was forthcoming in providing me with information for my paper on central banking.

After a while my father went to visit Ali Attiga, then director of research at the Bank of Libya, to tell him that I was back from the United States and was looking for a job. My father had previously met him in connection with writing an article for a magazine he was in charge of editing at the Ministry of Agriculture. At that time he mentioned to Ali I was about to arrive back home from the United States. Ali showed interest and asked my father to have me call for an interview. A week after the interview I was offered a job as an economist in the research department. I was delighted with the opportunity. I had been home close to two months and I was about to explore job opportunities in Kuwait and other Gulf countries.

Besides several Libyan economists there were two Arab expatriates in the department who were hired from the United States. One was Sadoun Hamadi, a college friend of Ali, and the other was Usameh Jamali. They were both from Iraq and like me each had a story to tell.

Iraq had a bloody revolution in 1958 led by army officers Abdel Karim Qasim and Abdel Salam Arif. The leading members of the royal family, King Faisal and Crown Prince Abdel Ilah, were executed. The Prime Minister Nuri al Said was killed during the disturbances. He had embarked on an unpopular foreign policy, including alliance with Britain through participation in the Baghdad Pact and opposition to the establishment of the United Arab Republic (U.A.R.) between Egypt and Syria. Conflicts among the officers developed. Arif championed the Pan-Arab cause and advocated Iraq's union with the U.A.R. Qasim rallied forces against Arab unity, mainly Kurds, and communists. He stressed Iraq's own identity and the need for internal unity. Soon Arif fell from power. To divert attention, Qasim advanced Iraq's claim to Kuwait's sovereignty, which brought him into conflict with Britain and Kuwait as well as other Arab countries. He also introduced major policy changes in the oil sector, which did not please the foreign oil companies. By 1963, Qasim's hold on power weakened. One faction of the army allied with the Ba'ath party started a rebellion and took over control of the Government. Qasim was executed.[13]

Shortly after I began to work in the Bank Sadoun was put in jail for allegedly being an active member of the Ba'ath Party trying to form cells in Libya, which was against the law. He fell ill in jail and was then asked to leave the country. The last time I met him was in 1967 in Damascus when he worked with the United Nations and I with the International Monetary Fund. Later Sadoun became a notable member of the Ba'ath party in Iraq and was appointed foreign minister and after that the speaker of the national assembly of Iraq. After the American-led invasion of Iraq in March 2003 Sadoun, like other senior members of the Party, ended up in a concentration camp where he spent over nine months under horrible conditions. One of my relatives who knew Sadoun's family told me that the tent where he stayed was jammed with a large number of prisoners and that he was given two blankets, one to sleep on and the other to cover. At night when he needed to go to the bathroom he had to jump over sleeping prisoners and walk through the mud, then come back to sleep with dirt over his feet and legs.

After seven months of incarceration he became ill with cancer and managed to speak with the commander of the camp. He asked about the charges that had been made against him, particularly since his name was not part of the published list of officials wanted by the occupying power. It transpired that one Iraqi informant was responsible for making allegations for the arrest. The commander was impressed with Sadoun's background. Sadoun had graduated with a Ph.D. in economics from the University of Wisconsin and I heard that the commander hailed from Wisconsin. Sadoun was released in the middle of 2004. He went to Jordan and Germany for treatment that was paid for by relatives but died in Qatar in March 2007 in his mid seventies. He left behind many good friends who remember him as being a Pan Arab nationalist, a humble and honest person.

Usameh Jamali worked for a few years in the Bank of Libya. We became close friends. His father, Mohamed Fadhil al-Jamali, was a former Prime Minister of Iraq and a former United Nations representative. After the revolution in 1958 Usameh's father was put in prison, but was released under pressure from the international community. He moved to Tunis to teach at the university. Usameh together with a friend, Mufid Jabbour, and myself drove to Tunis for a short vacation and were entertained by Usameh's parents. It was a pleasant trip and Usameh, Mufid and myself started to spend a lot of time together.

I was happy with my work at the Bank of Libya. I lived with my parents and enjoyed being close to the family again. My father's salary was barely sufficient to cover rent, food and other family expenses including Salwa's education in Damascus. Our income rose with my salary and we started to look for a larger apartment. I found one with four bedrooms and two baths in a new building near the American Embassy. I took my mother to see the apartment and she liked it, particularly being on the fourth floor with a large living room and balcony. The large entry room had a window overlooking the Mediterranean from a distance and the roof had a commanding view of parts of the city.

The dirt road leading to the apartment ended in a cul-de-sac facing one-story Libyan homes with open space in the middle. On both sides of the road were modern four-story apartment buildings. An auto-body repair shop occupied the first floor of one of the modern buildings opposite ours, and emitted continuous banging noises that took time to adjust to. In the back of the building was an empty space used as a stable for donkeys that brayed morning and evening, and triggered a chain reaction by dogs that barked and howled in the night. The noise level increased when the road was paved and opened up for traffic at the expense of losing the traditional homes that had to be torn down. We gradually adjusted to the noise level and enjoyed the apartment. After a few months I bought a new car, an Italian Fiat, which supplemented my father's old Renault that continued to need major repairs.

My brother Sidqi found an apartment in an adjacent neighborhood, and we saw a lot of him, Sana and Aunt Fakhriya who lived with them. Every Friday we all ate lunch together and enjoyed his review of discussions he had with his Libyan friends regarding social and political developments in Libya and the Middle East. He also discussed religious matters, books he read, and personal affairs in detail. Most of the time we were on the receiving end and thoroughly enjoyed his conversation. Sidqi had found his niche.

Besides teaching secondary school Sidqi gave public lectures about Palestine and the need for its liberation, published articles in the daily newspaper, and led an active social life with his close Libyan friends who were politically conscious of the need for political and social reforms. At one point he and his friends, who had established a liberal newspaper, were under close watch by the authorities. Sidqi was summoned by the security services and was asked to be careful or else he would be at risk of deportation.

Soon after the head of the newly established Palestine Liberation Organization (PLO), Ahmed Shukairi, visited Tripoli and offered Sidqi to join him in the newly formed PLO as an executive director. The Arab League created the PLO in 1964. Sidqi and family, which had expanded to include baby Muzna, moved to Jerusalem to take up the new job. Their departure left a big void in our lives and was very hard on my mother who now, once again, had two of her sons away.

My office hours at the bank were from 7:30 AM to 2:30 PM, Saturday through Thursday. My first job in the research department was to finalize a paper on inflation in Libya that was drafted by Sadoun Hammadi who had by then left the Bank. I also worked with my Libyan colleagues on the monthly economic bulletin that included statistical tables and analysis, and wrote articles for the bulletin. I wrote a study on public finance in Libya since independence in 1952, which was published in English and Arabic. Ali ran the research department smoothly and was highly respected.

Before Sadoun left the department he got married to a Palestinian young lady whose family came from Jaffa. Her father, Fawzi Kayyali, taught my brother Mahmoud mathematics at our secondary school in Jaffa. When Sadoun fell ill while in prison my mother and sister Salwa went to visit the family to express concern and inquire about Sadoun's health. Ali was visiting at the same time. I had earlier chatted with Ali about Salwa's education in Damascus and how demanding her English course was, judging from a paper she sent us in the mail. Ali had planned to go to Washington for the IMF and the World Bank annual meetings, and to visit Chicago where my brother Mahmoud and Ninon were living. Ninon had left a ring in our apartment during her visit a few months earlier and we thought Ali's upcoming visit to Chicago would be an occasion to return the ring to Ninon.

I invited Ali to visit us in our apartment. During his visit Ali met Salwa for the first time. After he returned from the United States Ali talked to me expressing interest in asking for Salwa's hand in marriage. I said we would be honored and I would be happy to convey the message. After discussing the engagement proposal Salwa and my parents said yes. A few months later, in June 1963, Ali and Salwa got married.

Ninon came with Samir and Aida to Tripoli to visit us in 1962 after she had been in Syria away from Mahmoud for two years, a period marked by grief, frustration, and anguish. When she traveled to Syria Ninon was pregnant and she planned to give birth in Latakia near her parents. Mahmoud intended to join her the following year after he finished his graduate studies in physical chemistry at the University of Chicago. They had hoped that Mahmoud would find a job in the petroleum industry in Syria or Qatar. The plans went awry. To begin with Ninon entered Syria on her Syrian passport, which included Samir and Aida. The Syrian authorities said she could not include the children in her passport because their father is Palestinian, and the children, like their father, are Palestinians under Syrian law. Children had to take the nationality of their father.

Five months after her arrival Ninon gave birth prematurely to twin boys, Rami and Fadi. Because of inadequate facilities, particularly a lack of incubators at the hospital, the twins passed away, one after three days and the other after one month. This was devastating for Ninon, Mahmoud and our whole family. When could a woman more need the love and support of a husband than when she has lost two babies and Mahmoud was unable to come to her.

Mahmoud asked his employer, Nalco Chemical Company, where he now worked full-time after graduation, to sponsor him for permanent residency in the United States. They did, but because he was born in Palestine his application for residency had to be considered under the quota of Israel with an expected waiting period of two years. Because his application for residency was in the pipeline, under United States Immigration Law he could not bring Ninon back to the United States. Under these stressful circumstances Ninon went to the American Consulate in Aleppo and got United States passports for the children. She then tried to get an exit visa from the Syrian authorities to go to Libya. The authorities confiscated the children's passports but did give her Syrian travel documents for the children because their father is a Palestinian. When she arrived in Tripoli Ninon was shaken and distressed.

The next day I went to see the First Secretary of the American Embassy whom I knew. I told him the story of Ninon. He was very sympathetic and asked me to bring the children's American birth certificates in order to issue new passports for them. The next day I gave him the certificates and while I was waiting he issued the children new passports and stamped Ninon's passport with an entry visa for the United States, which made the rest of Nino's short stay in Tripoli a restful and tranquil one, albeit full of excitement in anticipation of her soon joining Mahmoud in Chicago. In the rush before her departure Ninon left her wedding ring behind, but the ring eventually went back to her with Ali Attiga.

The residency problems and lack of passports have caused much suffering and anguish among the Palestinians. I have experienced the feeling myself. As I mentioned above, in 1952 my Syrian travel document was issued for one year and I could not renew it in Tripoli because there was no Syrian embassy or consulate at the time. My Libyan travel document, renewable every year, was not good for travel to some European countries, e.g. Switzerland, because I was a Palestinian.

While in secondary school and even among educated Arab friends I was told that the Palestinians are partly to blame for being refugees because they sold large blocks of land to the Jews, parroting the Zionists' propaganda that spread widely. Only recently has this propaganda lost its credibility with the publication of several books showing that the overwhelming majority of the land held by Israel was a result of Israel's policy of occupation and outright expulsion of the Palestinians.[14]

Let me tell you what happened to me: I went to the Israeli Embassy in Washington to ask for a copy of my birth certificate, which had been lost. I told the officer in charge I was born in Jaffa, Palestine and I needed a copy of the certificate. The officer said there is no Palestine, and no Palestinians, repeating what Golda Meir, a former prime minister of Israel, had publicly stated.[15] I told the officer Jaffa is occupied by Israel and it should be easy for the consulate to contact the municipality there. She would not listen.

I needed the birth certificate for my United States permanent residency application. In place of the birth certificate I had to get a notarized affidavit from a relative who was present in our house when I was born. Luckily my brother Sidqi in Cairo was able to ask Hasiba Dajani (an aunt of Sana, his wife) to make the required statement in Arabic, which was notarized and translated into English. It was then taken to the American Embassy in Cairo for certification. The American Embassy sent two of its Egyptian employees to my brother's house to talk to Aunt Hasiba. Facing two strange persons Hasiba got intimidated and wanted to alter the statement but my brother was able to convince the two employees that the statement was correct and that they should sympathize with the old lady who was approaching ninety years in age.

After the affidavit was approved by the Embassy my brother asked his daughter to take it to the neighborhood post office to put stamps on it and send it. At the post office she gave the clerk the money for the stamps and assumed that he would send the envelope the same day. After a few weeks I contacted my brother and told him the affidavit had not arrived and pressed on him the urgency of the matter. He had to redo the process from beginning to end and then he himself took the envelop to the post office and sent it as registered mail. What an experience!

When I first arrived in Tripoli Sidqi and his group of close friends wanted me to join the group, but I felt a little out of place. One day two of his friends came to call on me. I was just leaving for the beach with a new neighbor who worked for the United States embassy. I introduced her and said we were going to the beach. That was enough to make Sidqi's friends give up on me. Alice and I used to walk some way before reaching a bicycle rental shop. We rode the bikes to the Beach Club and back. Sometimes Khalil drove us to the beach. A few months later Alice transferred to Benghazi. At the Beach Club I met Hope, a Dutch schoolteacher working for Shell Oil, who loved to swim and we became friends. Many of the members of the Beach Club were Italians and other Europeans. I decided to run for the election of the board of directors and won, much to my satisfaction. The beach itself was delightful with its clean raked sand, a few little rocky pools and sparkling clear water. You could see fish darting around everywhere. There were also occasional jellyfish, to be avoided at all costs. The Club served an excellent lunch and dinner.

In the winter months we worked in the afternoon after a two-hour break for lunch. In the evenings I often took a long stroll on the cornice, which I enjoyed in all seasons. It was dotted with palm trees, with the harbor on one side, the old Tripoli castle, the Grand Hotel and the Uaddan Hotel and a few attractive apartment buildings, built during the Italian colonial period, on the other side.

In 1962, I went to Jordan to try to apply for citizenship and a passport. Jordan was the only Arab country that opened a wide door for the Palestinians to obtain Jordanian citizenship. I told Awni Dajani, a relative, who worked as an advisor to the King of Libya and later as an advisor to an American oil company, about my upcoming trip. He gave me the address of his brother in Amman and wrote a note on the back of his personal card to the Minister of Interior, Kamal Dajani, introducing me and asking him to give any help needed. I arrived in Amman from Cairo without a visa. I showed the immigration officer the card addressed to Kamal Dajani and he let me in.

After I arrived in the hotel the officer called me to say that the Minister had been contacted and I was allowed to stay. He added that the Minister would like me to call on him in his office the next day. I went to visit the Minister and explained to him my need for a passport. He asked his administrative assistant to immediately fill in all the necessary papers for citizenship as he was going to attend a cabinet meeting that day. At the cabinet meeting my application was approved and the next day I got a Jordanian passport. It was like a miracle. The next day Awni's brother and his wife invited me to dinner. I told them about life in Tripoli and the meeting with Minister Kamal Dajani who had acted quickly on my behalf. Normally, getting citizenship, after meeting all the requirements, took several months.

In 1963, I transferred to the newly established banking control department of the Bank. I was appointed assistant bank controller under a new director, on loan for a fixed period from the State Bank of Pakistan. Circulars went to commercial banks in both Arabic and English informing them of the new requirement for detailed reporting of loans and advances granted to their major customers. An inspection nucleus was established with two qualified staff members. Several months after the department was established, a Barclays Bank manager, who was anxious to get information about loans provided by other banks, sent me one of his staff to find out if I could do some translation work for him, which was like testing the waters for offering a bribe. I went to the deputy governor and told him what happened. He summoned the person from Barclays to his office and reprimanded him.

Once the new department started to function smoothly, the director became difficult to deal with and he picked fights with me and with his superiors. I transferred back to the research department. A team from the International Monetary Fund (IMF) was visiting the Bank at that time. One of the members, Franz Drees, came to my office several times to discuss financial statistics, which were needed for their report. He suggested that I apply for an economist's job with the IMF and said he would get me an application form. He was as good as his word and a few days later I filled out the form and sent it to Washington. Little did I know what a significant step I had just taken, one that would be a milestone for my career.

On that IMF mission were other members whom I got to know well in future years, particularly Said Hitti who has become a long time friend.

Ali Attiga whose transfer to the ministry of planning had come to an end returned to the research department. I told him about having sent an application for employment to the IMF. He suggested that I send a copy of the study I did on public finance to John Gunter, the head of the Middle Eastern department, and he said he would follow it with a letter of recommendation. I was lucky that the IMF had just begun to expand its lending operations and several newly independent countries had become members. I was hired as an economist in the Bureau of Statistics. None of this would have been possible without having my Jordanian passport.

Soon after, I got married to Sheila Whitehead whom I had been dating for two years. I met my future wife Sheila in October 1962, at a party given by my friend Mufid Jabbour, who was manager of Arabia Insurance Company. The party was held at the company's citrus grove on the beach near Tripoli. There were about thirty people. Mufid's girl friend had invited several of her English friends, including Sheila.

After a hearty barbecue lunch and drinks I went to talk to Sheila who stood out as a flower with pink petals. She told me she was working as a legal secretary at American Overseas Oil Company. She had recently arrived in Tripoli and was staying with friends until the company found her an apartment. I asked her if she would like to have a stroll on the beach. We walked and talked. Sheila was born in Eltham, a suburb of London, England. Her father, Arthur Whitehead, and mother Alice Whitehead were born and raised in South East London where many of their relatives lived. Sheila's younger brother, Christopher, was still in school. Arthur held an administrative job in a large industrial company and Alice was a stay-at-home mother. After graduating from grammar school Sheila went to business school for one year. Her first job was as a secretary to a stockbroker in the City. She left after one year to take a job with an export/import company.

I told Sheila who I was and what I did and we seemed to hit it off nicely. Sheila was twenty-three years old and I was twenty-eight. After the party we drove to the Beach Club where we played a round of ping-pong.

The next day was a holiday and I told Sheila that I, my friend Usameh and his girl friend, who was visiting from the United States, were planning to go to Leptis Magna, the site of famous Roman ruins about fifty miles from Tripoli, and wondered if she would like to joins us. She said she would. We enjoyed the trip a great deal.

Sheila in 1962

Sheila and I began to see each other frequently. We had a group of friends with whom we mixed regularly. Usameh and Mufid and their girl friends were particularly close.

One afternoon Usameh and I were almost swallowed by the waters of the Mediterranean. As we were swimming several hundred yards away from the shore the water started to swell; the shore and everything on it were covered by as much as twelve feet of water, which reached the top of the wall that separated the club's green grounds and tennis courts from the beach. It took a while for the water to recede and we swam back to shore unharmed. We did not lose our cool but were surprised and shaken up by what happened. The story might have been different if we had been swimming in shallow water. It was a dangerous tidal surge. The people on the outside deck of the clubhouse, Sheila among them, watched aghast and eventually retreated inside. There was nothing anyone could do and no higher place to move to. There was a sucking sound as the water pulled back, the beach with up-turned chairs and shades reappeared. Usameh and I started waving to show we were all right. The sun was shining; it was hard to believe anything had happened.

Taher in 1962

Soon after we met, Sheila came to my home for lunch. She loved my mother's cooking, particularly the stuffed grape leaves and squash, kibbeh (burghul ground to a paste and shaped into oblong balls and stuffed with spicy meat and onions), and sfeiha (dough patties topped with ground meat). As the days and months went by we fell in love. Sheila lived and worked in our neighborhood. She shared an apartment with three other British secretaries and her office was a couple of blocks from my family's home. I used to wave to Sheila every morning on my way to work whenever I saw her standing at her office window, and most of the time she was. She started work earlier than I did. We went on vacation by car to Tunis, Abusaid beach and Monastir with its attractive whitewashed houses, blue window shutters and lovely flowers. We also went to the Island of Djerba (in mythology the Island of Lotus Eaters) with its beautiful beaches and sand dunes.

Sheila became familiar with the way we lived and enjoyed listening to brother Sidqi's conversation at the dinner table. We enjoyed going on drives and picnics and having dinner with friends and sometimes going to parties. Usameh was a great party giver. As Sheila's two-year contract with Amoseas neared its end she decided not to renew it and to go back home. By that time I had an offer to work with the IMF in Washington. I asked Sheila if she would like to live in Kuwait where I had found a job. She said she would. I then told her about the offer of the IMF and asked her if she would marry me. She said yes. I broached the subject of marriage with my family. My mother and Salwa showed reservations because of the difference in culture and background. My mother said Churchill had divided our country into pieces and caused our disaster in Palestine. After discussions they left it up to me.

The marriage contract was drawn up with brother-in-law Ali representing Sheila and my father representing me as tradition called for, with Sidqi and some of his friends standing as witnesses. The dowry was a nominal sum that needed to be entered in the legal documents as consideration for the contract. We had a small wedding on October 23, 1964, in my parents' apartment. We invited one of Sheila's girl friends and some of my relatives. Sheila wore Salwa's wedding gown, as there was no time to have one made. It was not possible to buy a readymade gown. I gave Sheila a beautiful ring, a star sapphire surrounded by diamonds, which she treasures to this day. It was purchased from a rather wonderful Indian emporium on Istiklal Street where we often browsed looking at all the oriental goods. My parents and sisters gave us a nice party and a photographer came over for the occasion. My mother had arranged a delicious buffet for when the formalities of the marriage contract were over. All our favorites were there: kibbeh, spinach pies, sfiha and of course a wedding cake and an array of sweets. We spent the next few nights at Libya Palace Hotel, walking distance from the apartment. The day after the wedding we had a private dinner/dance for our friends at the Beach Club.

Taher and Sheila at the Beach Club

Sheila departed for London at the end of October. I followed Sheila a month later and stayed with her in her parents' house. Sheila's parents invited their close relatives for a party to celebrate their daughter's marriage. Arthur had five sisters and one brother, and Alice a brother and sister. Although they were scattered all over London and the South of England most of them came with their children, all eager to examine the "foreign" addition to the family. Sheila has always felt particularly close to her cousins Sylvia and Joyce on her father's side and June on her mother's side. We enjoy seeing them on our overseas trips and traveling together when possible.

I believe the party was a success even though it was difficult for me meeting everyone at one time. Sheila's Uncle Lew, a sports reporter with a newspaper, was very lively, thumping out popular tunes on the piano—none of which I knew! Sheila's brother, Christopher was 18 at that time and had just started at Canterbury University studying economics. He had long hair, much to my mother-in-law's horror and drove a scooter, which he kept taking apart in the front yard, making an awful mess. He came home for the weekend to join the party and shortly after that was home for the Xmas break. I had previously spent time with Chris in Tripoli when, as a student in high school, he made an adventurous trip through Europe, overland through France and Spain and then flying to Tripoli.

One person missing from the celebration was Arthur's second to youngest sister, Ivy, who had chosen to immigrate to New Zealand as a young woman. She married there and had two children, Alison and Paul. They all visited us in Washington and Kabul, Afghanistan and we were lucky enough to later visit Alison in Sydney and Ivy and Paul in Auckland.

At the time of our marriage in 1964, Sheila's parents were around fifty years old and their own parents had all died at fairly young ages. Alice's mother was killed when her home in London was bombed in 1942 during the war, whereupon her father came to live with them in Eltham. He succumbed to pneumonia ten years later and Arthur's father followed soon after of the same illness during one of London's deadly smogs. Arthur's mother had been the first to go in 1939, dying of breast cancer. Her youngest child, Jean, was only ten at the time. Alice's father had a streak of adventure and romance having followed the girl he loved to Canada and marrying there. They were homesick for London and returned two years later bringing a new baby with them (Alice's older sister Joan). Perhaps Sheila's sense of adventure came from them leading her to venture to Libya and a new life.

For a few days we did sightseeing in London and then we hired a car and drove on a rainy foggy day to an old inn in Bogner Regis on the South

Coast. This was our second honeymoon, the first being in the Libya Palace Hotel as mentioned. The Inn had delicious food and although the weather was cold and blustery we had an enjoyable few days. We went to the theater and concerts in London and to the cinema locally and also did quite a bit of shopping getting ready for married life in America.

6

Washington

We left for Chicago on December 27, 1964, on a Pan American flight. The IMF authorized the issuance of first class passages for our trip as was customary in those days. We were also allowed to ship our household belongings within a certain weight limit. As newly-weds our shipments from Tripoli and London were not large. We were the only passengers in the first class cabin. The captain came to talk to us and after hearing we were newly married presented us with a bottle of French champagne. Mahmoud came to the airport in Chicago to pick us up. Samir and Aida were with him. It was Sheila's first meeting with Ninon and Mahmoud. We spent a few days with them. We celebrated the New Year at a party they organized at their home. Sheila did not feel well most of the time and thought she might be pregnant.

We flew to Washington on January 2, 1965, and checked into the Francis Scott Key Hotel, walking distance from the IMF. It was a moderately priced hotel that someone in personnel at the IMF chose for us. It was later purchased by George Washington University and converted into student dorms. It was not the greatest introduction to life in Washington as the hotel was old and shabby and had no restaurant facilities. With Sheila feeling nauseated most of the time (not just mornings) it was a wonder we ever got anything to eat although I made good use of the excellent Fund cafeteria at lunch times.

I reported to work on January 5. The job at the bureau of statistics was technical and specialized. Like the rest of the IMF, the staff of the bureau came from different countries and there were economists and statistical clerks from the United States, Columbia, Cuba, Japan, Iceland, Korea, Egypt and Jordan. At the helm were the director and his deputy (both

United States nationals). The director was a pipe smoker and had a strong personality. The deputy was a little unkempt, quiet and hard working with a German accent. Under them were three division chiefs: one from Italy who specialized in trade statistics, the second from the United States and the third from Panama; the latter two dealt with financial statistics. I was assigned to work on country financial statistics published monthly by the IMF in International Financial Statistics (IFS). Before the end of the year I was asked to go on a mission to Lebanon and Pakistan that lasted six weeks. I was excited at the prospect.

I was given time during the day to look for an apartment with the help of one colleague and found a furnished one in South Arlington where the rent was less than in Washington. There was a bus service to 12th Street and Pennsylvania Avenue and a connection to 19th Street. Most of the time I had to walk in the freezing January cold seven blocks to the IMF because the connection time schedule was not what I needed to reach the office on time. I remembered my drive to work in Tripoli, which took ten minutes, but I kept saying to myself the walk was good exercise.

We stayed in the furnished apartment for one month. Sheila's sickness continued and she lost a lot of weight but remained resilient and took care of the daily shopping and cooking. There were shops right across the street making it easy to go out daily for supplies. We bought a used car from an IMF staff member who was being assigned overseas and started to look for a nicer apartment. We soon found one in the River House near the Pentagon. It was on the 14th floor with a great view of Washington. The drive to work was about 20 minutes long and I got a parking space in the IMF building. It was a convenient and subsidized arrangement that continued until I left the IMF, although the fees rose gradually.

The time had come to buy furniture for the apartment. Our new friends, Said and Angela Hitti, recommended an excellent place. Said who hailed from Lebanon, was a member of an IMF mission that visited Libya when I was there. Our family friendship grew and continued. We splurged on a king-size bed and matching pieces and some attractive dining and living room furniture. It must have been good quality as our younger daughter is still using pieces of the furniture. We had few acquaintances in the

Washington area but several of my colleagues were very kind and helpful, having us over for lunch or dinner, giving advice and generally showing us the ropes.

An American friend directed us to a doctor for Sheila, the months passed and Amira was born on August 23rd 1965, at Alexandria Hospital. We were thrilled with having a daughter. Being a first baby the labor was about 10 hours long and I sat at the hospital all day waiting for the news. Amira was born at 5 PM and weighed 8 lbs 1 oz. The Alexandria Hospital had some nice private rooms and Sheila was happy not to have to share. In fact she said the worst part of the whole experience was listening to a very frightened teenager screaming her head off in the next delivery room. The hospital stay at the time was four or five days. Lots of flowers and gifts arrived as well as visitors. Once again our new circle of friends made sure we felt at home.

I took Sheila home to the River House on a Friday morning, made her salad for lunch and left for the office. Neither of us knew a thing about babies and there were no parents around to help. However, we had the weekend to adjust and life soon settled into a new pattern. I had taught Sheila to drive during her pregnancy and she took the test four weeks before her due date. The policeman doing the test drive appeared the more nervous of the two. I gave her driving lessons on a road between our apartment building and Crystal House. The road was considered rural at that time. Later the whole area was built up and came to be known as Crystal City and the Pentagon Mall. During one of our lessons Sheila drove rather fast and hit the curb causing major damage to the steering column necessitating expensive repairs and staying without a car for a week. At this point we still only had one car. For pediatrician appointments I would leave Sheila the car and once again take the bus, which luckily was easy from the River House as there was a regular service.

Our day-to-day schedule was disrupted in late October 1965, when I was asked to participate in a six-week mission to Lebanon and Pakistan. Sheila thought it was a good idea to travel to Chicago with the baby during my absence. By this time Ninon and Mahmoud had three children: Samir (ten years), Aida (nine years), and Lina (one year). So Ninon already had her hands full. But she coped lovingly with a new mother and baby, and Sheila had the chance to become closer to Ninon and Mahmoud. Towards the end of this time my sister Khawla arrived in Chicago prior to taking up her studies at American University in Washington. Sheila, Amira and Khawla traveled back to Washington together.

The director of the Middle Eastern department headed the mission to Beirut, Lebanon. I attended several of the policy discussions held with the Lebanese authorities but my terms of reference called for a thorough review of monetary and government budget statistics and to discuss with the Lebanese officials the need to have the statistics sent regularly to the IMF Bureau of Statistics. The work was interesting and the head of the mission was well organized and kind. I went with him one afternoon to look at some charcoal drawings by George Corm and each of us bought a drawing of an Egyptian village girl. The artist had lived in Egypt in the 1940s. The drawing still hangs on our living room wall and is a great favorite. I wish I had bought both drawings, as they would have made a stunning pair.

When I arrived in Lebanon at the start of the mission, I was truly excited. I had flown first-class, as I would do on all my business trips. I checked in at the famous St. George Hotel overlooking the Mediterranean. Two days later I moved to the Phoenicia Hotel where the rest of my group was staying. The views of the sea and the mountains from my room were breathtaking. Everything about Beirut was fascinating.

I traveled on my own to Karachi, and Islamabad, Pakistan where I spent more than two weeks working on improvements to Pakistan statistical data published in IFS. The Bank staff was hospitable. A luncheon with department heads was given in my honor and one weekend the head of the research department of the State Bank took me out on the town early in the morning to see a live show of a snake charmer who had a basket full of snakes and we watched one snake go into a fight with a mongoose. We then went to the bazaar to look at local agricultural and other products. After lunch we went to see the film El-Cid with Charlton Heston. The outing made a welcome break.

On my flight from Karachi to Islamabad only a few passengers were in the first class cabin. The front seat was occupied by the then Foreign Minister ZulFikar Ali Bhutto who was dictating memoranda to his secretary during most of the flight. The other passengers were Pakistani women who seemed to enjoy the meal that was served. I was fascinated to see two of them put some of the butter served on their cheek and rub it into the skin. A source of vitamins, I suppose, or perhaps dry skin.

As foreign Minister, Bhutto asserted a foreign policy course for Pakistan that was independent of United States influence. He established stronger relations with China, made Pakistan an influential member in non-aligned organizations, and developed closer relations with Muslim countries such as Indonesia and Saudi Arabia. Bhutto became president of Pakistan in 1971, and also held the position of prime minister for several years. During this period he founded Pakistan's nuclear program, which was a major cause for the deterioration in his relations with the United States. Bhutto's political career came to an end when he was accused of having authorized the murder of a political opponent. Following a controversial trial, which was seen as politically motivated under the directives of General Zia-ul-Haq, Bhutto was executed in 1979.[16]

After my return to Washington I wrote a paper on the improvements I suggested in the monetary statistics of Pakistan. The division chief made several drafting changes and sent the paper to the head of the department for approval. The latter crossed out all of the changes made and wrote on the paper "This is an excellent and well written paper and should be published as PIFS (Papers on International Financial Statistics) for distribution in the Fund and to member countries." I started to feel more settled. My first mission was over and my first paper published.

During this period our social life became somewhat active. As mentioned, my sister Khawla was staying with us while completing her graduate work at American University. Looking for a house had become urgent as our apartment had only one bedroom. After some searching we settled on a house in a neighborhood called Waynewood (near Mount Vernon) that was close to a bus route. This was essential for Khawla as her schedule did not always coincide with mine and there was always the possibility of mission travel. She depended on me for rides to town.

We were invited to the homes of several of my colleagues at work and Sheila met with neighbors in the River House who became life-long friends. One afternoon on our way to see the house with Khawla, who had Amira on her lap, I crossed 23rd street in Arlington and was hit by another car. It was my fault. The police came and finding Amira unresponsive rushed her to the hospital fearing she might have had a concussion. Luckily she and all of us escaped injury. The other driver also was not harmed. It was a nasty scare.

Money became tight after purchasing a house on Croton Drive but we managed. We had nice furniture from the apartment in the River House and all we needed was a bed for Khawla, which we got on sale. Khawla started her courses in biochemistry and found a part time job at the lab in the chemistry department of her college. One day a secretary from the lab called me in the office to tell me that Khawla had splashed acid into her eye and had been rushed to Sibley Hospital for treatment. I jumped out of my chair and headed to the hospital. The doctor told me he was able to remove the outer layer of the white of the eye that was damaged, and had it not been for her lab partner who had immediately forced her head into cold water to wash out the eye, the injury would have been more serious. Khawla was in good spirits and recovered quickly.

Khawla's courses went very well. She became friendly with another student by the name of Sue Bonn, who lived near the university and who invited her to spend the night in case of need. Sue came on a visit to Tripoli after she and Khawla graduated and took jobs, Khawla in Tripoli and Sue in Nigeria. Sue was Jewish and smart. When she arrived in Tripoli she was handed an entry form, which included an item "your religion." She filled in "free thinker."

We entertained my Fund colleagues at weekends and also some of our neighbors and friends. Khawla was a great addition to our family circle and helped Sheila a lot, particularly with Amira who became very attached to her Aunt.

In 1966, my second year with the Bureau, I went on a mission to both Liberia and Sierra Leone in West Africa. Liberia, which means "Land of the Free", was founded as an independent nation by the American Colonization Society in 1847, with the support of the American Government, for formerly enslaved African Americans. The settlers referred to themselves as "Americans" and dominated the native population.

On the first working day after our arrival in Monrovia the four-man mission went to pay a courtesy call on President Tubman at the Mansion where he lived and worked. We went to Mrs. Tucker's office, the chief of staff. She took us to the waiting room and introduced us to the American Ambassador who was waiting to see the President. After a short while we were asked to go in leaving the Ambassador to wait. It was clear the President was not happy with the Ambassador who, by the way, was an African-American and had held high positions in the State Department before his appointment to Liberia.

The President was sitting behind his elegant desk puffing on a big cigar. We shook hands and sat in front of his desk after he said to us "have a seat." The head of the mission was shy and reserved and remained silent for a while. All we could hear was the sound of the President puffing on his cigar. Then came the sound of the door being opened and a large man in a smart suit, shining shoes, and large cufflinks entered. He was Mr. Johnson, the Acting Secretary of the Treasury. The President had fired the Secretary the previous month. Mr. Johnson with a low voice apologized for being late saying the traffic held him back. The President smiled and said "have a seat." Then there was a period of silence and more puffing on the cigar. Mr. Johnson broke the silence by saying in a booming voice, "Mr. President the IMF mission is here to pay their respects." In response the President took a long puff on his cigar and said, "I haven't heard them say anything yet." The head of the mission got the hint and explained briefly the task of the mission and the meetings the mission hoped to have with government officials. Then he highlighted some problems in the Government budget, particularly a large deficit and a high level of defense spending. The President puffed long on his cigar and said the mission could come here and suggest reducing expenditures in general but it has no business telling us where the cuts should be. There was silence again. The head of the mission started to speak about another area, which pleased the President.

As we were leaving, the Ambassador was asked to go in. Liberia was a strategic place for the United States with its location in West Africa close to some socialist states like Nkrumah's Ghana and Sekou Toure's Guinea. Moreover, it had the Firestone Rubber Plantation, iron ore concessions, and the Voice of America station. The Ambassador later died of a heart attack in Monrovia and it was rumored he died in bed with a Liberian woman.

After the departure of the mission I stayed behind a few days to discuss ways to improve the flow of financial statistics to the IMF. I walked the main street alone; I felt a bit awkward, as I was the only Caucasian person in the street. A young woman on the other side of the street walked topless as they do in the interior of Liberia.

I left Monrovia by air for Freetown, Sierra Leone and completed a similar mission. An IMF consultant from the United States headed the research department of the Central Bank and there also was an IMF representative, who was British. I worked long hours with the staff of the Bank and the job was completed in one week. There was a pleasant tea break every afternoon when the Governor of the Bank invited senior staff to join him for tea. The English tea service was very elegant with expensive china and linen napkins. The tea break provided the Governor with the opportunity to exchange views with the staff in a relaxed atmosphere. I was impressed. I was also invited to have lunch with the director of research and other senior staff and had dinner with the IMF representative at his home. The latter also invited me to join him and his family for a picnic at the beach over the weekend, which I did. My visit to Sierra Leone was really enjoyable.

Upon my return the governor sent a letter to the director of my department thanking him for the technical assistance and praising my work and dedication. I was very happy to read the letter. A few days later I called on the division chief in charge of Sierra Leone in the African department. The IMF Representative had told me while I was in Freetown that the division had a vacancy for an economist. I told the chief that I was interested in the position and gave him copies of the papers I had written on financial statistics in Pakistan and Sierra Leone and my college paper on central banking.

It did not take long before I transferred to the African department. Knowledge of the French language was important for joining the African department so in anticipation of any potential transfer I had lessons in French for a few months and Sheila had some knowledge of French and helped me tremendously in my early lessons.

The deputy director of the African department in charge of personnel was from France. In my interview with him, which went well, I spoke in English but was careful to say a few sentences in French that I prepared for the occasion. My interviews with other senior staff of the department also went well and I was told that the department had asked for my transfer. However, to be completed the transfer process required the approval of the director of the bureau where I had worked for over two years. He was not happy. He called me to his office to discuss the reasons behind my request for a transfer. I said I was happy in my job and that I was proud to be a member of his staff and the only reason for my request was to gain experience in area department work to prepare for a banking career back home. I was successful in appeasing him and getting him to approve my transfer.

I was delighted to get a transfer to the African department. I was assigned to work on Ghana whose government under Kwame Nkrumah had just been over thrown by a coup d'etat while he was on his way to visit China. Nkrumah was well known internationally and together with Seiko Toure' of Guinea and Julius Nereiri of Tanzania, they were the heroes of independence from British and French colonialism. They, together with Gamal Abdel Nasser, inspired and led the wave of socialism in Africa. My first mission to Ghana was to be preceded by travel to Damascus, Syria to discuss problems in IFS statistics with the staff of the Central Bank.

I spent ten days in Damascus. I visited my Uncle Khalil and family and other relatives. Some of my old acquaintances from Latakia had become influential in the government and I spoke to some of them on the telephone. One of them, a cabinet member, showed up with an entourage at a restaurant in Bloudan, a suburb of Damascus, where officials of the Central Bank were giving me a farewell lunch. He greeted me warmly and we talked briefly hoping to see each other again. I was leaving Damascus the next day.

My visit to Damascus took place a few months after the Six Day War, which started on June 5,1967. Again Israel prevailed in the war. It launched a preemptive attack on Egypt, citing Egypt's announced closure of the Straits of Tiran (the opening from the Gulf of Aqaba to the Red Sea) to Israeli shipping and other provocations. Israel's fighter jets caught and destroyed nearly the entire Egyptian air force before it could get off the ground. In similar strikes Israeli warplanes destroyed a large part of the Syrian and Jordanian air forces. The preemptive strikes brought air superiority to Israel and enabled it to decimate numerically superior Arab ground forces and to seize the Sinai Peninsula, the Gaza Strip, and the West Bank (including East Jerusalem). In the course of the war a large number of Palestinians were displaced, some for a second time. My feeling of shame over this disastrous defeat was overwhelming. Six months later U.N. Security Council Resolution 242 was passed, confirming the inadmissibility of the acquisition of land by force and calling for Israel's withdrawal from occupied territories, the right of all states in the region to live in peace within secure and recognized borders, and a just solution to the refugee problem.[17]

In his book "The Fateful Triangle" Noam Chomsky, the noted Jewish American intellectual, quoted Menachem Begin, the former prime minister of Israel, as saying, "In June 1967, we again had a choice. The Egyptian army concentration in the Sinai approaches do not prove that Nasser was really about to attack us. We must be honest with ourselves. We decided to attack him." Yitzhak Rabin, Israel's former chief of staff, was quoted in Le Monde of February 1968 as follows: "I do not think that Nasser wanted war. The two divisions he sent to the Sinai would not have been sufficient to launch an offensive war. He knew it and we knew it."[18] This goes to dispel the propaganda that spread in Western press at the time of the 1967 War that the Arabs were the aggressors and Israel was only defending itself.

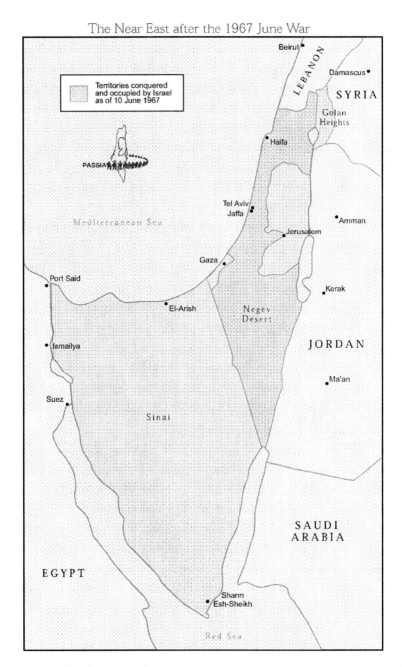

The Near East after the 1967 June War

Territories conquered and occupied by Israel as of 10 June 1967

Source: Palestinian Academic Society for the Study of International
Affairs (PASSIA), Jerusalem. Reprinted with permission of PASSIA.

From Damascus I traveled to Accra, Ghana by air via Cairo and Nigeria. In preparing for the mission in Washington I was asked by the division chief to draft a briefing paper for the mission. I had to stay late in the office to work on a paper I had no clue how to do. I searched the files and was able to find helpful information for the briefing paper. Sheila was not happy with my staying late in the office and would urge me by phone to close up and come home. She drew the line at missing family dinner. With all my travels there were too many times when I was apart from the family. Anyway the mission to Ghana went well, and I was happy to get home after an absence of three weeks.

In the following two years I traveled to Ghana many times as the IMF began to play a major role in rearranging the country's short-and medium-term debt to other governments, international banks, and foreign suppliers. The debt, in excess of $800 million had accumulated during the Nkrumah era as a result of poor investments. Many of the development projects that were implemented were not economically feasible. For example, foreign suppliers built so-called white elephants, including cocoa silos that would store large quantities of cocoa to influence the world price. The silos proved useless under the weather conditions in the country. A chocolate factory had to be abandoned for the lack of demand in the local market and inability to compete internationally.

I traveled several times to Accra and London in connection with the debt rescheduling, a subject embarked upon for the first time by the IMF. I also helped the staff of the Bank of Ghana in working out detailed estimates and scenarios for the rescheduling exercise with the Soviet Union. In addition I participated in Aid Meetings in London for the purpose of providing the country with long-term loans and grants to help Ghana meet her debt burden inherited from the previous regime.

During some weekends in Ghana the mission took time to do some sight seeing. We visited Volta Lake and Akosombo Dam, the port of Tema and Kumasi where we met with the Ashanti King, the Asantahini. At his palace, where beautiful peacocks were strutting around in the grounds, the Asantahini received us with wide smiles and offered us glasses of French Champagne. We also went to Bolgatanga in the Upper East Region of

Ghana. Colonel Afrifa, who had become the de facto leader of the country, provided us with a military helicopter for the trip. We also saw the old castles near Accra built by the Portuguese, which served as an embarkation point for the slave trade before crossing the Atlantic to Europe and America.

On one of my early missions to Ghana my daughter Zena was born. It was April 23,1968. I received a cable from the IMF telling me of the news. I was surprised because Sheila had told me the due date predicted by the doctor was early May and on that basis Sheila and I decided that I should not turn down the mission. Luckily we had wonderful neighbors who took Sheila to Alexandria Hospital. They left home about 10.00 PM and our second daughter was born at 5.00 AM the next day. Khawla was at home with Amira. I arrived in time to bring Sheila from the hospital.

On my visits to Ghana I often used to stop in Tripoli to visit with the family for a few days. On one of these trips one of my colleagues wanted to stop with me in Tripoli on the way from London in order to visit the Roman ruins at Subratha and Leptis Magna near Tripoli. So we spent a few days in Tripoli. We stopped on the way to take pictures of a small camel caravan that was passing by. Camel caravans, men riding donkeys with panniers of fruit and vegetables on either side or pulling small carts are still common sights in the Middle East.

My assignments in 1968–69 also included missions to Zambia and Algeria. Before independence Zambia was part of British Rhodesia, which included Malawi and Zimbabwe. On the way from London to Lusaka, Zambia, members of the mission stopped in Nairobi, Kenya where we visited the famous National Park, rich in wild life. We hopped on a station wagon before sunrise and were taken deep into the park to see lions, tigers, giraffes, zebras, and monkeys. I took a lot of pictures and was awed to see a lion tearing to pieces a smaller animal and sharing the prize with his lioness and cubs. I was beginning to know Africa well, north, east, and west.

The work of the mission to Zambia was demanding. We collected statistics on the major sectors of the economy, analyzed each sector, discussed our analysis with officials of the government and wrote a final statement summarizing the mission findings and policy recommendations that was delivered to the Minister of Finance the day before our departure. We stayed two weeks in Zambia. Over the weekends we visited an animal park sanctuary that had hippos and elephants. We also flew to Victoria Falls, the largest in the world, and spent one day sightseeing. The Falls are probably one of the most amazing sights seen on my travels. Upon returning to Washington the mission spent several weeks preparing the report on the economy of Zambia, which after it was discussed by the Board of Directors was sent to all the member countries of the IMF.

In September 1969 I went on a mission to Algeria. On the way the mission members stopped in Nice, France, and spent a night in a fabulous old hotel in the city. The discussions with the authorities in Algiers were in French and most people I came in contact with in Algiers spoke little Arabic having been brought up under French Colonial rule, which lasted from 1830 to 1962. The colonists had modernized the economy but lived apart from the Algerian majority, enjoying social and economic privileges. A widespread nationalist movement against French rule created the seeds for the war of independence during 1954–62, which was marked by terror and violence. France granted Algeria independence, and most Europeans left the country. Although the influence of the French language has remained strong, since independence the Algerian authorities have made major strides in regaining Algeria's Arab and Islamic heritage.

The head of the mission was highly intelligent but he loved to drink and crack jokes. One evening we had dinner in the hotel's open air dining area. He sat near a Swedish woman whom he had met earlier and whose husband was on a trip outside Algiers. After several drinks he got carried away and I saw his hand stretch down over the woman's leg without hesitation. I could not believe my eyes. The woman took it lightly and luckily she did not make a scene realizing he was drunk.

During the mission, we heard on the radio that on September 1, Libyan military officers led by Colonel Gaddafi staged a coup d'etat against King Idris I while the King was in Turkey for medical treatment. The monarchy was abolished and Crown Prince Hasan Senussi was placed under arrest. My parents and sisters were in Tripoli. My brother-in-law Ali was a cabinet minister and I worried about him and his family. I could not reach him or my parents by telephone and had to wait until we got back to Washington to hear their news. Luckily they were all safe. However, Ali Attiga and Awni Dajani were jailed together with prominent figures of the previous regime but they were released after about two months. Ali was later appointed Chairman of the Libya Insurance Company, and after that he moved with his family to Kuwait to take up the position of secretary general of the Organization of Arab Petroleum Exporting Countries.

The year 1969 also saw Yasser Arafat becoming the Chairman of the PLO, with headquarters in Jordan, after his Fatah group and its paramilitary wing emerged as the best organized among the groups making up the PLO. The following year Arafat became the supreme commander of the Palestine Liberation Army, the regular military force of the PLO. My brother Sidqi left the PLO executive committee in 1969 but continued to be a member of the Palestinian National Council. From 1977 to 1984 Sidqi was again appointed a director in the executive committee of the PLO and a member of the Palestinian delegation to the United Nations.

In 1970, tensions between Palestinians and the Jordanian Government increased greatly as Palestinian militias began taking control of several strategic positions in the country. On September 15 of that year, the Popular Front for the Liberation of Palestine, a faction of the PLO, hijacked five planes and landed three of them near Amman. After the passengers were moved to other locations, three of the planes were blown up. The Jordanian Government moved to regain control and King Hussein declared martial law. Fighting erupted between the Jordanian army and the Palestine Liberation army with Syria supporting the Palestinians.

Both the United States and Israel showed readiness to aid Hussein if necessary. In an attempt to negotiate a peaceful resolution to the conflict President Nasser led an emergency Arab League summit in Cairo in September 1970, but attempts to reach an agreement between the two sides failed. President Nasser died of a massive heart attack hours after the summit. Shortly thereafter the Jordanian army achieved dominance and inflicted heavy casualties upon the Palestinians.

Arafat managed to enter Syria with nearly two thousand of his fighters. They crossed the border from Syria into Lebanon to join Fatah forces in that country, where they set up new headquarters. By 1975 the PLO became a force to reckon with in Lebanon and became involved in the Lebanese civil war between Muslims and Christians, taking the Muslim side. During this period the PLO continued to wage its guerilla warfare in northern Israel from its bases in southern Lebanon, which eventually led Israel to invade Lebanon and occupy Beirut after carpet bombing from the air and shelling from the ground. Syria, whose army went into Lebanon in 1976, participated in the war and sustained major losses, particularly of its aircrafts.

The PLO was forced to evacuate Lebanon in September 1982, moving its headquarters to Tunis. Syria tightened its control over Lebanon, and a new political Islamist Shiite movement backed by Iran appeared on the scene. At the same time the Lebanese Christian Militia (Phalangists) who were allied with Israel went into a rampage at two Palestinian refugee camps, Sabra and Shatila, killing hundreds of Palestinians, men, women and children, encouraged and incited by Israeli military officers of the highest rank. Later investigation by Israel found that Ariel Sharon, the defense minister, was indirectly responsible for the massacre.

The period after the expulsion from Lebanon was a difficult one for Arafat and the PLO. But soon Arafat's hand strengthened following the Intifada (uprising) in occupied Palestine, which directed world attention to the plight of the Palestinians. In 1988 in a speech at a special United Nations session held in Geneva, Switzerland, Arafat declared that the PLO renounced terrorism and supported the right of all parties concerned in the Middle East conflict to live in peace and security, including the state of Palestine, Israel and other neighbors. The prospects for a peace agreement with Israel brightened but suffered a setback when the PLO supported Iraq in the Persian Gulf War of 1991. Thereafter negotiations were held in Norway, which led to the Oslo Accords of 1993. The agreement included provisions for Palestinian elections, which took place in 1996, and Arafat was elected President of the Palestine Authority.[19]

7

Monrovia

In the summer of 1970, the position of resident representative in Liberia became vacant. I knew the IMF representative who was stationed there and he filled me in during one of his visits to Washington on the work situation and living conditions in Monrovia. I asked Sheila if she would like us to live in Monrovia for a year or two. She was excited at the idea of an overseas assignment in Africa. I applied and was selected for the position. On the way to Monrovia we spent a few days in Geneva, Switzerland where Amira developed a fever. We called a doctor with the help of the hotel. The doctor examined Amira and gave us a prescription to reduce the fever and assured us it was safe to travel the next day. We left for Liberia as scheduled. We checked in at Monrovia's Ducor Intercontinental Hotel, which was built on a cliff overlooking the Atlantic Ocean on one side, the city and the river on the other.

It was August, hot, steamy with lightening and thunder and sudden massive downpours of rain. Electricity service was erratic and I remember us getting stuck in the hotel elevator one day when the power went off. It was totally, utterly black, not one glimmer of light showing. I still smoked at the time so I flicked on my lighter and somehow it was a comfort to get a glimpse of each other and the other passengers. It took the hotel about 10 minutes to get the emergency generator going by which time we were all feeling warm and sticky and, I think, somewhat scared. The relief was enormous when the power came back on.

We stayed in the hotel until my predecessor vacated the house rented by the IMF. The two-story house was on the outskirts of town close to a rocky beach and to the houses of the Egyptian ambassador and Stephen Tolbert, brother of the vice president, who later became minister of finance. The Catholic hospital was also nearby. Amira was five-years old and Zena two-years. Sheila found a kindergarten school for them, which was run by a woman from New Zealand. We kept the house help and the night guard employed by our predecessor. The Government provided me with an official car and a driver; our private car arrived later from Washington.

After calling on the Secretary of the Treasury to introduce myself I went to the Mansion to pay my respects to President Tubman. At the meeting I spoke briefly about the strength of the Liberian economy and areas that might need continued attention like external debt, expenditure control and the improvement of the revenue collection machinery. I referred to the IMF special relations with Liberia and assured him I would do my best to strengthen the relationship. President Tubman expected everyone to dress formally. Official functions called for tuxedos or morning coats and at garden parties it was definitely hats and long gloves for the ladies, regardless of the heat.

Liberia used the United States dollar as its national currency. Its main exports were rubber, iron ore, and diamonds and the budget relied heavily on revenues from the Firestone Rubber Plantation, iron ore concessions, and ship registry under the Liberian Flag. My work revolved mainly around monitoring the cash flow of the Government through the Bank of Monrovia, a subsidiary of City Bank, and providing technical assistance to government departments, including in the process of budget preparation and implementation.

The Secretary of the Treasury was a trained economist. He used to come to work late and stayed in the office until after midnight. Once in a while he called for meetings at about 10:00 PM to discuss Treasury matters with the expatriate auditors stationed in the Treasury, and to draft memoranda and letters of understanding to the iron ore concessionaires. Whisky was served nonstop. He was good at drafting but by the end of the meeting four hours later he looked drained and drunk. I was invited to some of those night meetings but after attending two I apologized. He did not like it and our relationship became a little strained. I mentioned to Sir Robert Jackson, a former high-ranking official of the United Nations and advisor to President Tubman, during one of his visits, about my strained relations with the Secretary of the Treasury and explained to him the background. I knew he would pass the information to the President.

A week later Sheila and I received an invitation from the President and Mrs. Tubman to join them on a trip to Cape Palmas, the President's birthplace. It was an overnight trip by sea on the President's luxurious yacht, previously owned by actress Elizabeth Taylor. We spent one night on board the boat and one night in the President's executive mansion and were made to feel most welcome. We enjoyed the trip except that Sheila got seasick and had to leave the dinner table and go to the cabin. The seas along West Africa are notoriously rough and Mrs. Tubman always liked to sail within sight of the land, which did not help matters.

On the way back we flew on a tiny and rickety plane over a dense jungle and were concerned about whether we would make it. Our New Zealand friend who ran the kindergarten was taking care of Amira and Zena. The next morning Monrovia's English language newspaper carried the news of our trip with the President. It was meant to highlight the importance attached to the job of the IMF representative. It was the first and only time Sheila had agreed to travel with me without the kids. Zena was seventeen-years old and Amira was in college before Sheila traveled with me on an IMF mission. To qualify for a free trip with her husband a wife had to accumulate two hundred points, one point for every day the husband was traveling on business. Sheila had many hundreds of unused points.

A few months after our arrival in Liberia President Nasser of Egypt died of a heart attack at the age of fifty-two. We were shocked by his sudden death, which provoked a collective mourning in Egypt and other Arab countries. World leaders attended the funeral in which an estimated 4 million people took part. In Liberia there was a large Lebanese business community who shared the grief over the death of a popular Arab leader. The Lebanese owned the largest supermarket, automobile dealership and gold jewelry shops in Monrovia. I used to see some of them at the Treasury building tracing their unpaid bills, the accumulation of which in the past had caused a problem for the Treasury and encouraged kickbacks and corruption.

Many items were flown in from Lebanon every week, in particular some fruits and vegetables not available in Monrovia. Among the delicious local produce were bananas, papayas and pineapples, which were sold by native women outside the super market. A clamor arose whenever a foreigner arrived in his/her car, and Sheila found it advisable to always go to the same vendor who would rush forward yelling "my customer, my customer" so that the others would pull back.

We had an active social life in Monrovia and were often invited to diplomatic receptions and other private parties. We also threw parties for our friends and whenever an IMF mission visited Liberia. The secretary of the treasury was invited to our official cocktail parties, but he came close to midnight accompanied by one or two of his secretaries/girlfriends. His wife never came with him, which reminded me of my Ghanaian friends in Accra who would come to visit me at the hotel with a girl friend tagging along instead of their wives whom I had met when visiting their homes. It was considered prestigious to have a girl friend in tow.

Monrovia had a large British community and Sheila became friendly with a number of Britishers whom I met through work or whose children went to the same school as Amira and Zena. We also made friends with Arab families from the United Nations and business communities. We used to go to the beach over the weekends and on the way back and forth Amira and Zena would sing their favorite songs and Sheila would sing along. I pretended to sing with them but they knew I did not know the words. Elwa Beach, about half an hour away, was protected by rock barriers and as such was considered safe, but Cooper's Beach, a little further on, was treacherous with strong crosscurrents, and several drownings were reported every year. When we went to Cooper's we swam in a large lagoon adjacent to the beach to be on the safe side, although we were nervous that the water might contain parasites.

Monrovia has a tropical climate with heavy rainfall and violent thunderstorms, particularly in the rainy season. Electricity went down during the storms and we had to suffer extreme humidity without the benefit of air-conditioning. The telephone lines also frequently went down either because of the storms or sometimes at the whim of the repair people who wanted to earn extra money on the side. I became expert in finding them on the road and having them repair the lines that connected to our house. Of course a few dollars baksheesh helped a lot. We had a few chances to explore the interior including a visit to Firestone Rubber Plantation and to tribal villages where we saw national dances and witchdoctor ceremonies.

Our first R&R (Rest and Recuperation) trip was to the Canary Islands. We spent one week each in Las Palmas and Tenerife. Besides sight seeing and going to the beach we decided to rent a car and go up to the dormant volcanic mountains of Tenerife. The car was an old British Triumph and we discovered while on top of the mountain that the breaking system was not functioning well and almost fell off a steep slope as I was backing up to turn around. We descended the mountain carefully on second gear and made it safely. Down on the beaches the temperature was in the 70's. For us coming from Liberia it felt quite cool and we walked around wearing sweaters in contrast to the Germans and Scandinavians who were very scantily clad—mostly in bikinis. Up on the mountains there was snow.

During the vacation I had to write a paper on national saving for an economic conference in Monrovia scheduled to begin soon after the end of the vacation. It was painful and caused me a great deal of anxiety. The paper had to be reviewed by my supervisor in Washington. It was well received at the conference, save for some criticism by an economic advisor to the President. That year I was promoted to senior economist.

During the second year in Monrovia, we went on home leave to Tripoli and were very happy to be part of Tawfiq and Khawla's wedding. Amira and Zena were bridesmaids along with some of their cousins and my mother organized speedy trips to the Italian dressmaker to make them very pretty satin dresses. Of course, my mother used the same tailor regularly for all her clothing. She had very smart dresses and suits; the Italians were very talented in the arts of fashion and sewing. There were a few shops in Tripoli with ready-made clothes but my mother preferred to choose her own materials, which were always of superior quality, and to discuss the style that would suit her best. There were a large number of guests at the wedding and I got the chance to see several of my friends.

My adopted sister Bashira who had graduated from the University of Libya at Benghazi got married two years later while we were in Washington. Bashira's husband Mohammad Shatta, hailed from the Sudan. He was a journalist and a political activist and in later years he sought and was granted political asylum in the United States. Mohammad and his family live near Chicago.

On the way to Tripoli we visited Morocco spending a week in Rabat, Casablanca and Fez. In Casablanca we hired a taxi and asked the driver to take us to a public beach and to return at a certain hour to pick us up. It was a hot day and the beach was packed but we enjoyed the water and were able to buy some snacks and drinks. To our great relief the taxi showed up on time. We were pretty far out of town and I am not sure what we would have done if he had let us down since we did not see any taxis around.

The hotel in Rabat was palatial with marble floors and beautiful inlaid tables surrounded by oriental cushions. We had some wonderful Moroccan food. A group of well-known Egyptian musicians dined in the restaurant at the same time, and we were told the musicians had been invited by the King to play for him in the Palace.

President Tubman passed away while we were in Tripoli. He was in the United Kingdom for treatment. The Vice President, Robert Tolbert, became President. He appointed his brother Stephen, a wealthy businessman known to be tough and ruthless, as Secretary of the Treasury. He did not have a background in finance or economics but luckily he appointed Ellen Sirleaf who had studied at the University of Wisconsin as an advisor. The Secretary and I got along well. I moved to a fancy office with a bathroom and shower. It had been occupied by one of the assistant secretaries whose position was eliminated as part of a major reorganization. Ellen Sirleaf, who in 2005 was elected the first woman president of Liberia, became a good friend. One day she invited me to go along with her and the Secretary of Agriculture on a flight over the mountains of Liberia where iron ore deposits were located. It was a small airplane with 4 seats. The Secretary piloted the plane over dense forests and small villages. The scenery was impressive.

At the end of the second year Sheila and the children left Monrovia for London a week ahead of me. Two days later the house was broken into while I was asleep. When I woke up I stretched out my hand to the bedside table to get my watch. It was not there. The radio wasn't there either and my wallet was missing. I called Isaac, our domestic helper from down stairs. He came up and we both puzzled over how the thief was able to get in without waking up our dog Wolf. The entry point we discovered was the next bedroom where Zena used to sleep. The thief climbed up to the window, removed the glass panes from the frame and jumped in. We found my wallet on the floor empty except for my Virginia driver's license. We checked my closet and the down stairs rooms and found nothing else was missing. Wolf, a German shepherd, wagged his tail and sought affection by licking my hand. He was trained to stay on the first floor and in the living room. Upstairs was out of bounds. We figured that the thief must have known this and someone must have told him. We suspected the night watchman who disappeared after the burglary. I reported the burglary to the Liberian authorities. Investigators came to the house and took samples of fingerprints found on the window and assured me of quick results.

That evening I decided to stay in the house and when I went to bed around midnight I dragged our dog Wolf upstairs to my bedroom and he slept on the carpet near the bed. At about two in the morning Wolf started barking and as I woke up I found him trying to push the curtain open with his head. I jumped up and opened the curtain over the door of the bedroom balcony and saw a naked man jump from the balcony to the ground. He had probably come back for my clothes. In the morning I decided to check into the hotel for the rest of the week. I could not face any more surprise visitors. I was able to get Wolf a nice home before I left Liberia.

Later, in April 1980, a military coup was staged by a group of noncommissioned officers led by Master Sergeant Samuel Doe. They killed President Tolbert in his mansion and rounded up and shot all the cabinet members and some influential businessmen. We were shocked. We had socialized and had dinner with many of them. Samuel Doe was the first Liberian head of state not a member of the Americo-Liberian elite. In late

1989, a civil war began and a year later Doe was ousted and killed. An interim president, Amos Sawyer, was appointed and in 1994 he handed power to the Council of State. Charles Taylor was elected President in 1997. His autocratic and dysfunctional government led to a new rebellion in 1999, which continued until mid-2003. He was forced to resign and accept asylum in Nigeria. In 2005 Ellen Sirleaf was elected Liberian president. Charles Taylor was later extradited from Nigeria and put on trial by a United Nations tribunal in The Hague for alleged war crimes during the civil war and crimes against humanity. His trial began in June 2007, and is continuing.[20]

8

Back to Washington

From Liberia I went back to Washington in July 1972. We had been away for two years. During this time we had rented our house in Waynewood and coming back was a good feeling. The girls were very excited and Amira still remembered the house. Our tenants had taken reasonably good care of it but we almost immediately began improvements, including putting in an extra bathroom.

Before I had a chance to adjust to being back in the African Department I was asked to prepare for a mission to Ghana, which was followed by missions to Uganda, Ivory Coast, and Mali. The last two are French speaking. I was not fluent in French but made up the deficiency by writing or editing major parts of the reports in English.

The mission to Uganda was conducted in a tense atmosphere. President Idi Amin who was most unpopular in the West ruled the country with an iron fist. Soldiers in their jeeps moved around the capital city of Kampala brandishing their weapons and stopping people at their whim. The mission members restricted their movements in the city going only to meet officials to collect data and discuss policies.

The Ministry of Finance officials in Kampala were not cooperative and did not provide us with the budget figures. I told the deputy minister that our work was being hampered by the lack of information. He said he had no authorization from the minister to release the data. The next day I was asked to see the Minister who said, "the first thing we do to those who do not cooperate with us is to send them back to where they came from." I said with a smile that we would be grateful if the minister would instruct his people to cooperate with us, and that we would very much like to stay in Kampala until we finished our job. We then talked for a short while about general subjects. The next day we received the budget data and my colleagues were able to collect the information on the economy that they had requested from other ministries and from the central bank.

In the hotel I saw a Libyan I had seen before. He owned an upscale store in Tripoli that specialized in women clothing. I invited him for a cup of coffee, and we had a chat. He told me he had been in Uganda for several years engaged in the coffee trade. He bought the coffee beans from small farmers and sold them to customers in Italy making a good profit. He knew all the important people in Kampala and they made it possible for him to buy at the most favorable prices. He invited me to have dinner with him at his home in Kampala. He lived alone in a large villa and carried a pistol at all times for protection. Before I left Kampala he invited me again with all the members of the mission and we had a sumptuous dinner at his house. The encounter made a welcome diversion from the bureaucratic difficulties we were facing.

On October 6,1973 another war erupted between Arab and Israeli forces, once again disturbing my peace of mind and increasing my anxiety. Syrian troops and tanks battled Israeli forces along the Golan Heights seized by Israel in 1967, while Egyptian forces retook key positions on the eastern bank of the Suez Canal and the adjoining Sinai Peninsula. However, a sustained counter attack by Israel, strengthened by United States airlifts of weapons, turned the balance in favor of Israel. Most hostilities ended on October 22, with both sides having suffered a large number of casualties. The war brought back world attention to the Arab-Israeli conflict. United Nations Security Council Resolution 338 secured the cease-fire worked out by Henry Kissinger through his shuttle missions. The Resolution called for direct negotiations between the parties concerned to implement Resolution 242.

The continued support of Israel by the United States during the war angered King Faisal of Saudi Arabia, who together with other members of the Organization of Arab Oil-Producing Countries (OAPEC) imposed a total embargo on oil shipments to the United States. The embargo also covered, with varying degrees, other countries depending upon the extent of their support for Israel. This was followed by production cuts, and a fourfold increase in the posted price of oil to $11.65 per barrel. The embargo, which lasted five months, is estimated to have cost the United States economy 500,000 jobs and a $10 billion to $20 billion loss in its gross national product. The impact on the economies of the European countries, and their subsequent change of attitude toward Israel in the United Nations was dramatic[21]

In the IMF, attention focused on oil producing countries in the Middle East and their increasing balance of payments surpluses and foreign reserves. The IMF started special consultation discussions with these countries with a view to recycling the surpluses through adjustments to domestic demand and other economic policies. These developments made me anxious to seek a transfer to the Middle Eastern department (MED) in order to go where the action was.

I spoke with the director of the African department about the possibility of transfer and he was receptive. My transfer happened quickly and surprised those in the IMF personnel department who were not involved in the initial request and had major difficulties at that time initiating transfers from one department to another.

I was assigned to work as the desk economist for Saudi Arabia and Yemen and I went on a mission to both countries. The work was interesting and I was excited to be visiting the two countries whose history is steeped in the culture of the Arabs.

During my first visit to Saudi Arabia I visited Mecca during the weekend and performed the Umrah, which is considered the "lesser Pilgrimage" compared to the Hajj. I wore a garment unique to the Hajj, consisting of two pieces of white cloth which cover the lower and upper parts of the body, and entered into a state of consecration known as ihram. Ihram signifies divesting oneself temporarily of all marks of status and individuality. All the pilgrims wear similar garments. I visited the Ka'aba and performed the prescribed acts of worship. The Ka'aba was originally built in antiquity by Prophet Ibrahim (Abraham) and his son Ismael as the first sanctuary on earth dedicated to the worship of the One God. Muslims face the direction of the Ka'aba whenever they perform salat (prayer). My great, great, grandfather Hassan Dajani (1816–1890) died and was buried in Mecca after performing the Hajj.

During another official visit to Saudi Arabia I performed the Umrah again. The morning of my scheduled departure from Riyadh on March 25, 1975, I woke up to the news of the assassination of King Faisal. The murder occurred at a majlis (sitting), an event where the King opens up his residence to the citizens to enter and petition him. The murderer was Prince Faisal Ben Musa'id, the King's half brother's son, who was captured after the attack.

He was tried and was found guilty. He was later beheaded in the public square in Riyadh. The King was succeeded by his half brother Khalid. I stayed in Riyadh an extra two days until the airport was re-opened.

In that year I co-authored an article on the oil economies of Saudi Arabia and Iran, which was published in Finance and Development and wrote an article on the economy of Yemen published in the IMF Survey.

9

Kabul

In 1976 a position for an IMF resident advisor in Afghanistan became open and I was selected to fill the position. The family and I spent two years in Kabul. For a while we lived in the Intercontinental Hotel until my predecessor left the house rented by the IMF. We enrolled Amira and Zena in the American School and they adjusted quickly and made new friends. Sheila did not seem to adjust as quickly. She felt closed in as the house had high walls around it and bare mountains in the distance with an elevation of 5,876 feet. Most women walking around wore a burqa, which covers the whole body and has a padded headpiece and a mesh screen in front of the eyes.

The house had a large front lawn and a swimming pool. It was located in an upscale neighborhood next to the American and Indonesian ambassadors' houses. The Jam Hotel was also a close neighbor. It catered to foreign tourists of the hippie type who were not well off and whose main interest was using drugs, mainly opium and heroin.

My office in Da Afghanistan Bank, the central bank, was on the second floor overlooking the town square where the ministries of finance and planning were located. A side door to my office connected to the research department. At my office door sat two elderly messengers who did little besides making tea. I worked closely with one of the deputy governors and with the staff of the research department who provided me with economic and financial data needed for analysis and for periodic reporting to the IMF. I also developed strong relationships with officials from the ministries of finance, planning and trade who were involved in policy matters and who participated in the annual consultation discussions with the IMF.

Afghanistan's economy is mainly agricultural. Its exports are wheat, fruit and nuts, hand-woven rugs, Karakul (infant lamp skin), precious stones and natural gas. In recent years opium-production and exports have increased substantially.

I worked hard in Kabul and kept the Middle Eastern Department informed of economic conditions and prospects in the country. When the IMF mission was in town Sheila and I gave a large party for them and often entertained them to lunch.

On weekends we went outside the city to scenic spots like Kargha Lake for picnics. We visited the Salang pass high in the Hindu Kush Mountains that connect the country with its northern neighbors. We also drove over rough roads to the great Bamiyan valley in remote northeastern Afghanistan where two statues of Buddha were carved in the cliffs. One of them, more than fifty meters tall, was believed to be the world's largest representation of Buddha. The sky was brittle blue and the early morning sun made the cliffs glow like embers. Later in 2001, the Taliban government decided that the statues were offensive to Islam and ordered their destruction despite pleas from international organizations and several countries including Pakistan and Egypt, both Muslim. The historical statues exist no more.

The lakes of Bandi Amir near Bamiyan were stunning in their blueness and clarity. They sprang up from the ground and added luster to the desolate surroundings. We stayed overnight in Bamiyan in a yurt, a round cottage with a straw roof. All night long we could hear mice scurrying over our heads through the straw. It was quite un-nerving but we were told by our friends in Kabul to expect the night visitors. The "hotel" comprised about a dozen yurts. There was a large room where simple dinners and breakfasts were served. The elevation is 8,376 feet, much higher than Kabul and one really felt on top of the world.

We went on short vacations to the city of Kandahar in the south and to Peshawar in Pakistan driving through the treacherous and famous Khyber Pass where many British soldiers in 1878 were trapped and killed during the British-Afghan War. The scenery was breathtaking and filled one with awe. We almost had an accident on one of the tricky turns over the pass.

Before we reached Peshawar we passed by tribal areas where all kind of weapons were offered for sale in the open market. In Peshawar we stayed at Dean's Hotel, which had been built by the British during colonial days as a resort in a cooler area of the country. The hotel retained some remnants of grandeur and was an interesting place to stay. As always we had to be very careful where and what we ate but if we needed a change from the hotel there was a good kebab restaurant nearby. For our girls the highlight of a trip to Peshawar was a visit to a large bookstore that stocked up on English books and comics. We also loved to go to the area where copper pots were made and we bought several attractive and decorative items. We purchased small hand-woven rugs and folding leather chairs. The streets of Peshawar were teeming with people, bicycles and donkeys not to mention a few cars.

We had good friends in Kabul. Among them were Saleem and Marwa Kutob. Saleem was a laboratory expert with the United Nations. They had four children, the two girls being close in age to Amira and Zena. We had many happy times. We frequently had dinner in each other's homes and went on picnics together. I hired an Egyptian professor at Kabul University to teach Amira and Zena Arabic. In the past I had given them lessons on weekends and they made progress and seemed to enjoy it. The girls did not take to the teacher. So we asked Saleem's older daughter, Nadia, to teach the girls, and the arrangement was successful. Sheila became a member of the Diplomatic Wives Association and was asked by the British ambassador's wife, who was president at the time, to serve as secretary of the Association. This involved writing the minutes-quite an ordeal when many of the members did not speak fluent English, especially the Russian ambassador's wife who, according to Sheila, always had a lot to say.

We also had social contacts with some Russians. Sheila and I were invited by the economic advisor of the Russian Embassy to have drinks at his apartment. He was reciprocating our invitation to him and other Russian embassy staff to come to one of our parties welcoming the visiting IMF mission. His apartment, which was part of a huge residential complex housing the embassy staff, was rather humble. He and his wife were very welcoming and treated us to delicious Russian hors d'oeuvres and a lot of vodka. Every time he toasted us the glasses went up to our mouths and came down empty, except for Sheila's glass, which she managed to control tightly. As the invitation was for 9:00 PM we ate dinner before leaving the house on the assumption that we were having drinks only. This proved wrong, as the Russian hostess had prepared several delicious stew dishes, which were served at 10:00 PM. We talked in generalities and pleasantries. When I asked our host about the Soviet political system and the state of the Soviet economy, his wife raised the volume on the gramophone. It was clear she wanted to blot out the conversation.

During the first year in Kabul we went on a two-week R&R (Rest and Recuperation) vacation to Sri Lanka, Thailand, and Hong Kong where we got some flavor of South East Asia. We bought jewelry from both Sri Lanka and Bangkok and clothing from Hong Kong. We visited the De Mels in Colombo, Sri Lanka. Douglas was with the United Nations in Kabul and Esme, his wife, gave Sheila piano lessons. At the suggestion of the De Mels we went to a new beach resort in Ranweli. The air conditioning was not functioning and we had to open the windows at night, much to our regret as the mosquitoes came through in droves and kept us awake most of the night. There were mosquito nets over the beds but they were not sufficient. We also visited Kandi in the mountains where we stopped at a Buddhist temple and a zoo. We took turns in riding a big elephant near the central market. En route to Kandi as we climbed to higher, cooler ground we visited one of the many tea plantations for which Sri Lanka is so famous.

In Bangkok we took a bus to the beaches in Pataya on the China Sea in the south. The bus was full. On it were an Australian and his Thai girl friend. Both seemed drugged. The woman kept staring at Amira and Zena. She tried to lean across the aisle to touch Amira. Hideous scabs and track marks covered her arms and legs. This incident made a profound impression on my daughters, then eleven and nine years old, who were well aware that this woman's hideous appearance and abnormal behavior was the result of taking drugs. The man had an ugly new scar on his face starting on one side of his forehead and going across the bridge of his nose to the other side of his face as if someone had tried to slice his face in two. I stood up and told the driver to stop the bus and call the police. The Australian man moved the woman to the inside of the seat and gave her drugs to calm her down. Amira tells me this incident affected her for the rest of her life. She cannot even watch someone using heroin on television because of this incident, which was very upsetting to us all. The hotel and beach area in Pataya were beautiful and after such a rocky start we had a relaxing few days.

During our second year in Kabul we went to London via Tashkent, Uzbekistan, and Moscow staying a few days in each doing sightseeing. At the Soviet Embassy in Kabul where I got the visas for the trip I talked to the representative of Intourist Agency to ask for information about obtaining tickets in advance for the famous Bolshoi Theater in Moscow. The Soviet lady who spoke to me was called Mukarramah, a Muslim name which in Arabic means the one who is treated with respect and generosity; she informed me that it would be possible to get the tickets from the Intourist Agency in Tashkent and that Mr. Sayedof the head of the office would be able to help me. In Tashkent I went to call on Mr. Sayedof who immediately gathered three of his office staff to hear what I had to say. Evidently he was afraid of meeting a foreigner on his own because of the tight security situation in the Soviet Union at that time. Any way he said he could not help.

We toured Tashkent during the day and visited one of the large parks. Being summer it was extremely hot, over one hundred degrees. To my surprise a teenage-boy who saw me pull my pack of Dunhill cigarettes from my pocket said to me in Arabic these are "sagayer nafeesah" (precious cigarettes). I asked him where he learned the language. He said in the mosque school. In the 9th Century during the spread of Islam into Central Asia, cities like Tashkent, Samarkand and Bukhara prospered as trade and intellectual centers and many mosques and madrassahs were built in those cities.

In the evening we took a bus to the circus. We had asked the hotel receptionist to organize the tickets for us and once again an Intourist agent had to be contacted. They absolutely insisted that because my daughters then aged ten and twelve were half price we only needed three seats and two halves made a whole. Nothing we said would convince them that we had to have four seats. Luckily the circus tent was not full and the ticket collector had no problem when we only presented three tickets. Surprisingly we had a lot of freedom of movement going off on our own at night and taking the bus. We had thought that in a Soviet republic we would be closely watched and our movements restricted. The next day we went to a great ice skating show, which was visiting from Moscow.

The people were kind and generous. At the table next to us in the restaurant a large family was celebrating. They brought us a large basket of fruit, a touching friendly gesture. The problem was my wife was afraid to have the children eat it. She always avoided fruit and salad while traveling and stuck to well-cooked food. However, we did not want to cause any offense so bravely started peeling what looked the safest, such as apples.

The flight from Tashkent to Moscow was crowded and unsafe. Some passengers' luggage was placed in open overhead compartments, and cigarette smoke clouded the cabin. Children sat in their parents' laps and no one had seat belts on. In Moscow we had an organized sightseeing tour from the hotel, which covered all the famous sites. Much to our annoyance the Bolshoi Theater was closed for renovation. Under communism tipping in restaurants was not permitted. So I was surprised when the waiter serving us in the hotel restaurant pocketed the change from our bill and disappeared. The flight from Moscow to London was very organized and luxurious. The service was impeccable unlike the flight from Tashkent to Moscow. We came to the conclusion that the Soviets wore two hats, one for their third world republics and the other for the world to see. We did lots of shopping in England, visited with Sheila's family and rented a place at the seaside town of Eastbourne for two weeks.

The second year was easier and we felt very settled. Winters in Kabul were very cold. Two or three feet of snow could fall in one night and then Kabul was cut off from the world. The roads would be closed in all directions and the airport shutdown. Kabul's own method of snow removal would kick into action; men with large wooden shovels would line up about 6 abreast and the men trudged down the street pushing the snow before them. It was surprisingly effective. Every few yards the snow would be pushed to the sides of the roads where there were drainage ditches in place of sewer pipes. The piles of snow melted and seeped into the ditches, which were unpleasant and always abuzz with flies. Heating their homes was a great problem for the poorer Afghans, of whom there were many. All year they would save and store anything that could be used as fuel and one would see men with sacks slung over their shoulders walking the streets searching for litter and anything that would burn.

Our life in Kabul continued at an even pace until around noon on Thursday, April 27, 1978, when I heard shots and a few bomb blasts echoing in the area of the Presidential Palace near the Bank. I looked out of my office window and saw three tanks in Pashtunistan Square; there was a large crowd of civilians standing around the tanks but no sign of panic. I thought security forces were being readied to quell any demonstrations, as there were rumors the previous day that a large demonstration was likely to take place to commemorate the death of a leader of the communist party who was assassinated nine days before. His funeral was attended by hundreds of followers who made inflammatory speeches and shouted slogans against the Government. Several communist leaders were reportedly arrested.

On Thursdays we worked half a day and were off on Fridays. When I got home I told Sheila about the soldiers and the tanks that I saw on my way home though I thought we were in no danger. We ate lunch on the patio, as it was a cool spring day and our garden was bursting with color. While eating lunch the firing started and tanks with long gun turrets began rolling along our street. The air filled with clouds of black smoke. For the next hour there was heavy firing from all directions and soldiers battled their way into the Interior Ministry headquarters and also took control of the Post and Telegraph Office, the center of Afghanistan's civilian communications, both located on the same block as our house.

Our first thought was for Amira who was on the far side of town at the American School taking part in a convention with students visiting from Pakistan, one of whom was staying with us. Zena was at home. Almost immediately, before the phones went dead, we heard that Amira was at the house of an American friend whose parents we knew well. They took twenty extra children into their house located near the school and little did we think that it would be two days before anyone could move again. Luckily they had a freezer full of food and although they ran out of drinking water there was enough soda for everyone.

At about four in the afternoon supersonic jets went overhead breaking the sound barrier with a deafening sound. We thought the American Ambassador's residence next to us had been hit either accidentally or otherwise. In actual fact the Presidential Palace was being bombed and our house was in the direct flight path of the Soviet-made MiG-21s. For the next two hours we had to put up with horrendous noise and the feeling that a little mistake on the part of the jet pilots would eliminate us all. Our house was built with wide glass windows and no basement so we huddled under the staircase to take shelter and hoped for the best. In the evening I heard someone calling my name several times from behind the high wall that separated our house from the American Ambassador's house. It was the voice of one of the embassy staff. I went near the wall and answered the call. It turned out to be the father of one of Amira's friends. He had run out of cigarettes and wondered if I could spare some. I went in and got a pack and threw it over the wall. I asked him if he had heard any news from the family where Amira was staying. He assured me that all the Americans in that neighborhood were safe.

We moved Zena to our bedroom that night and went to bed as usual. At midnight we woke up to the noise of pitched battles and explosions, which lasted until 3:00 AM. We went back to sleep again and woke up at around 8:00 AM. Judging from what we heard from neighbors and friends we were probably one of the few families who were able to sleep at all that night. We listened to the local and international radio stations. Radio Kabul announced the overthrow of President Mohammed Daoud and "an end of the reign of the imperialists." Reports from other radio stations were tentative, but it was clear the tensions of Kabul reached from Moscow to Washington, from New Delhi and Islamabad to Peking. The United States and the Soviet Union had been competing in Afghanistan through economic and arms assistance. As long as Afghanistan pursued a neutral foreign policy the strategic problem that the country presented was not acute.

By Friday afternoon the curfew was lifted and people started walking in the streets looking at the soldiers and the big tanks. I had thought the town would be heavily damaged after the battle but the pilots and the commanders appeared to have been selective and well trained. Only a few of our acquaintances had nightmarish experiences as stray bullets and rockets hit their houses.

My driver came to pick me up on Saturday morning. He said he had to report to security officers at the Bank and would no longer be able to take our children for school sports at the United States Embassy field for fear of being implicated in one imaginary thing or another. Tanks and soldiers had blocked the area where Amira was staying but the roadblocks were lifted on Saturday so we were able to bring her home. Amira told us she was really frightened. Rockets hit a house nearby, and soldiers entered the house where she was staying to see what was going on.

During the first hours of the coup President Daoud and his family were lined up in the palace grounds and shot dead, bringing to an end more than two hundred years of the rule of the family of Nader Khan. Daoud had come to power in 1973 after deposing in a palace coup his cousin King Zahir Shah who was in Italy for an eye operation.

Immediately after the April 1978 coup a revolutionary council was formed and Nur Mohammad Taraki elected Chairman. The weeks after the coup were difficult. Every one in the Bank was tense and fearful, except those who were in the communist party or were sympathizers of the party. Our two-year assignment was almost up and we counted the days until the end of June when we said goodbye to our friends in Kabul. In the evening the muazen stood at the minaret of the mosque in our neighborhood to call for prayers. I heard the call again at dawn the next day before we left. I thanked God that my family was safe.

After our departure from Kabul political developments in Afghanistan continued to dominate the news. Major splits occurred in the ruling communist party and in October 1979, Taraki was secretly executed and Hafizullah Amin, known for his independent nationalist inclinations, became the new president. This did not go down well in Moscow and in a swift chain of events in December 1979, Amin was assassinated and the Soviet Red Army swept into Afghanistan. The Afghan ambassador to Czechoslovakia was flown in to take over as the new president. The Soviet occupation, which lasted nearly 10 years, was brutal and met with strong resistance by groups of Afghan and other Islamic fighters (mujahideen), including Ben Laden and his followers. Financial support and weapons flowed in with much covert assistance from the United States

In 1989, the Soviets withdrew, and eventually the mujahideen took over the reign of government but their victory was marred by infighting among the various factions. Towards the end of 1994, the Taliban emerged in the southern city of Kandahar and was gradually able to spread its influence over most of Afghanistan. The Western World reacted negatively towards the Taliban's extreme Islamic policies, and the United States tried to pressure the Taliban to give up Ben Laden but the pressure was resisted. After the suicide attacks on the World Trade Center in New York and the Pentagon in Washington on 11 September 2001, the United States and its allies began air attacks on Afghanistan and succeeded in sweeping the Taliban from power. An interim government headed by Hamid Karzai and backed by United States military power was sworn in but until recently has not been able to exert control beyond Kabul, the capital. The Taliban has lately reemerged as a fighting force and is now battling the government and NATO forces for the control of the country.[22]

During my two years in Afghanistan major political developments were taking place that would influence the peace process in the Middle East for years to come. The victory of Menachem Begin and his right-wing Likud coalition in the Israeli national elections of May 1977 represented a major triumph for those who oppose giving up any of the territories Israel had acquired during the 1967 War, especially the West Bank and East Jerusalem, and gave a strong push to the settlement movement in the occupied territories.

In January 1977 Jimmy Carter became the President of the United States. He moved to rejuvenate the Middle East peace process and played a decisive role in the success of the negotiations between Egypt and Israel at Camp David, which resulted in the signing of a peace treaty between the two countries in 1979. Under the treaty, Israel agreed to withdraw its armed forces from the Sinai in return for normal diplomatic relations with Egypt and guarantees of freedom of passage through the Suez Canal. At the same time, the United States committed several billion dollars of annual subsidies to both Israel and Egypt.[23]

The peace treaty had enormous ramifications on Middle Eastern politics. Egypt was seen by the Arab League as having deviated from the Arab ranks by choosing to relinquish its pan-Arab duty of liberating the occupied Arab territories, particularly Jerusalem, and of restoring the Palestinian Arab people's national rights, including their right to repatriation, self-determination and establishment of the independent Palestinian state on their national soil. Political ties between the Arab countries and Egypt were severed and Egypt's membership in the Arab League was suspended. On October 6, 1981, Sadat was assassinated and was succeeded by his vice president Hosni Mubarak.

My parents moved to Cairo in 1979, and lived near my brother Sidqi and his family. Sidqi used to stop by their apartment daily to chat at length about his social and political activities. Sheila and I also flew several times from Washington to visit with them. The home-leave trips were a very important part of our lives. They kept us in touch with our roots and allowed our daughters to know their grandparents and other close relatives. Both our daughters now enjoy keeping in close touch with their many first cousins (eighteen on the Dajani side and one in England). My parents came to visit us in Washington in 1980. We took them to the White House, the museums and to the Shenandoah Mountains. They also visited with old Palestinian friends in the Washington area. From Washington they traveled to Chicago to visit my sister Khawla and her family and to Tyler, Texas to visit my brother Mahmoud and his family. Both my parents died in Cairo away from their home in Jaffa.

10

Washington Again

Before I had time to settle down I was asked to go on a mission to Oman, which was followed by missions to Qatar, Bahrain, Yemen, and Afghanistan. I led the advance team to these countries and had major responsibility for writing the staff reports.

In a bureaucracy one is likely to have brushes with one's colleagues or bosses. In my case I was not satisfied with the rate of my promotion. I asked for transfer to the IMF Institute, the training arm of the organization, and the transfer was quickly arranged by the director of administration. The timing was right because the IMF management had authorized the Institute to introduce Arabic in some economic courses offered by the English division, so that trainees from Saudi Arabia and other Arab countries who were not fluent in English would be able to participate in such courses. An Arabic translation unit was established in the bureau of language services and translators/interpreters were hired for this purpose. All lectures and workshops had to be translated into Arabic and the interpreters had to get used to the English/Arabic economics vocabulary.

My first assignment after my transfer to the English division of the Institute was to write a paper for a new course in economic analysis, and to give a few lectures. I had just quit smoking at the insistence of my wife and daughters and writing the paper in the evenings and weekends without smoking was painful. Every time I had the urge for a cigarette I drank a glass of cold water, which was helpful. By the time I finished the paper, about three weeks after I had started, my addiction to tobacco came to an end. I was free after 30 years of having the bad habit. The paper was translated from English into Arabic, French and Spanish to be used by all the divisions in the Institute.

I began to lecture in English with two interpreters sitting in the translation booth. There were thirty participants in the course; they all had college degrees in economics and held senior positions in their countries. Of these, ten were Arabic speaking. My lectures went well, particularly as I drew on my experience in the field. I enjoyed interacting with the participants in the course. For the Arab participants the lecture summaries and the workshops material were translated into Arabic and I was given the responsibility of supervising what became known as the Arabic arrangement. There were teething problems, to be sure. The Arab participants found the earphones irritating after an hour of wearing them. They also found the translation of the lecture documents and the simultaneous interpretation in need of improvements. When they dealt with the administrative division, which looked after matters relating to their lodging, visits to a doctor, and organized sightseeing, they found problems to complain about. I was called upon to trouble shoot potential problems and to diffuse them when they occur.

As the Arabic arrangement functioned relatively smoothly and more Arab participants signed up for the courses there was talk of introducing more economics courses in Arabic and creating an independent division. In the Institute's budget submission to the IMF management for that year, a full-fledged Arabic division was proposed. Unfortunately, because of budgetary constraints the proposal was turned down. At that time Saudi Arabia and the Gulf countries were lending the IMF substantial amounts to strengthen its ability to meet the increasing need of developing countries for financial assistance. So I went to see the Saudi executive director who represented Saudi Arabia in the IMF and with whom I was friendly. I told him that without a push from the Saudi authorities for an expansion in training and for the creation of an Arabic Division the likelihood of approval by management was not strong. He wrote to the Ministry of Finance about our conversation and as a result the Saudi authorities sent a letter to the managing director of the IMF stressing the need for creating an Arabic division like the English, French and Spanish divisions. The managing director made a notation on the bottom of the Saudi letter instructing senior management to create an Arabic division.

When the Institute budget proposal was submitted, a division was born and I was promoted to division chief. I was satisfied that my efforts had borne fruit. Another very interesting and challenging time in my career was about to begin.

The Arabic division expanded rapidly. I helped to recruit a well-trained Arabic speaking teaching faculty all of whom had PhDs in economics. I interviewed one of them in Larnaka, Cyprus on my way back from Egypt where I was on a mission. He flew over for the interview from Abu Dhabi where he worked as a lecturer.

The work of the division and its reputation in turning out solid teaching material in Arabic helped to increase the demand for the courses. The material included a case study on Egypt, incorporating a number of workshops on financial programming and economic policy, which was published in a book that circulated widely in Middle Eastern countries.

The Arab Monetary Fund (AMF) based in Abu Dhabi, United Arab Emirates asked the IMF and the World Bank for help in establishing an economic policy institute. I was asked to go on the mission together with an economist from the World Bank and a professor from the American University of Beirut, Lebanon. Sheila came with me on the mission and we traveled to Jordan, Egypt, Sudan and Algeria. The mission lasted three weeks and the report that I wrote to management upon my return was circulated widely in the IMF. Soon after that the AMF Economic Policy Institute was established. Members of the Arabic division were periodically sent to Abu Dhabi to provide teaching assistance.

Sheila also came with me to Kampala, Uganda in 1985 when I headed an IMF Institute Seminar on economic policy in Uganda. At that time Uganda was emerging from a successful military coup, which toppled the Government of Idi Amin who sought asylum in Saudi Arabia. Heavily armed soldiers drove their vehicles around the town, and we were escorted to our hotel by a contingent of those soldiers who remained as guards during our stay. Huge bats were nesting outside on the windowsills of our rooms in the hotel. The hotel had a pleasant dining room in a separate building. The menu was limited but the food was quite eatable. On weekends we visited the market and government officials invited us to a resort outside Kampala where we spent the night. We also went to see the source of the White Nile at Lake Victoria.

I also headed IMF Institute seminars on macroeconomic policies in Jordan (1988) and Bahrain (1989) with Sheila traveling with me to both countries. Other seminars included those to Saudi Arabia (1989 and 1990), Indonesia (1990), Syria (1991), Georgia and Turkmenistan (1992), Egypt, Lebanon, Fiji and Turkey (1993), and Ethiopia (1994). During the latter year I also visited Turin, Italy to give a lecture on financial programming and economic policy at the International Labor Organization Institute. Several UNDP representatives posted in Arab countries attended the seminar, among others. On the way home from Ethiopia I stopped in Jeddah, Saudi Arabia to discuss with the Islamic Development Bank the possibility of co-financing IMF training courses in the Middle East, as the UNDP had already begun to co-finance IMF courses in several countries.

Taher at the podium in Jakarta

The mission to Fiji was particularly memorable and once again Sheila had a chance to accompany me. We flew via Los Angeles and stopped a couple of nights in Hawaii. From there we crossed the Pacific to Fiji. The airport was near the city of Nadi on the side of the island where all the tourist resorts were located. We had to take a small plane over to Suva the capital. Both the passengers and the luggage were weighed carefully and then the plane was loaded and balanced accordingly. It held only five passengers, all IMF economists, except for my wife Sheila.

As we flew over the jungle-like interior the Australian pilot took great pleasure in pointing out the wrecks of several small planes below. My wife said, "This is nerve racking." One of her priorities after our arrival in Suva was to enquire at the hotel about an alternative route to get back. We were able to hire a taxi to drive all the way around the far side of the island with most of the road running beside the sea, a much pleasanter experience. Sheila and I stayed in the resort area for a few days at the end of the mission to enjoy the beauty of the island.

On the missions to Ashkabad, Turkmenistan and Tiblisi, Georgia the IMF hired Russian interpreters and sound technicians who sat on all the lectures that we gave in English. All the participants spoke Russian. The interpreters were very efficient and one of them spoke Arabic, having worked at the Russian Embassy in Baghdad. In Ashkabad we were given a government guesthouse with a kitchen and a cook. One morning I noticed that the two Russian technicians had black eyes, swollen noses, and wounds on their faces. I asked the interpreters to tell me what happened. They said that the technicians, who were around 40 years old, had been drinking heavily the night before and got into a heated argument that ended in a fierce fight. However, they settled their quarrel in the morning before going to work so we carried on as if nothing had happened. For this mission I had to carry with me enough cash dollars to pay for the wages of the Russian interpreters and technicians. It was difficult after the dismantling of the Soviet Union in 1991 to conduct exchange transactions quickly through the banking system. I carried the cash in my money belt, which was risky but had to be done.

11

Palestine

My visit to Palestine in October 1994 came on the heels of major developments in the occupied West Bank and the Gaza Strip, which influenced the prospects of peace between the PLO and Israel. First, there was the Intifada, an Arabic word for uprising, which began in 1987 as a result of disillusionment on the part of the younger generation of Palestinians over the lack of progress in securing self-determination. The Intifada was fueled by the rapidly expanding Jewish settlements and the expropriation of land and property by the Israeli government. The harsh response by the Israeli military forces resulted in the death of a large number of Palestinians and focused world attention to their plight.[24] Secondly, the Gulf War in January 1991 between the United States-led coalition and Iraq resulted in the ejection of Iraqi forces that had invaded Kuwait; Arab countries participated in the war as part of the coalition. In September 1991, the United States convened a Middle East peace conference in Madrid to resolve outstanding issues between the Arab countries and Israel.[25] As little progress was being achieved in bilateral discussions between the Arab and Israeli delegations, PLO and Israeli officials held secret meetings in Norway in 1993 to hammer out what became known as the Oslo Accords.

The Accords called for the withdrawal of Israeli forces from parts of the Gaza Strip and the West Bank and affirmed the right of the Palestinians to self-government within those areas through the creation of a Palestinian authority. Palestinian rule was to last for a five-year interim period during which a permanent agreement would be negotiated and would cover major issues such as Jerusalem, refugees, Israeli settlements, security and borders.[26] In 1996 Palestinians held elections for president and for a legislative council. Yasser Arafat won by a large majority as president. In the following years negotiations did not settle any of the core issues, thus causing increased unrest among the Palestinians.

The purpose of my visit to Palestine was to discuss technical assistance from the IMF with the newly formed Palestinian authority, particularly in the area of training. Another economist came on the mission. This was a great opportunity. I had no chance to visit my boyhood home since 1948. The airport in Lud north of Jerusalem was crowded and immigration officials were busy interrogating some of the travelers, particularly those with Arab features. My colleague and I did not have any difficulty because we were on official business. We also did not have trouble crossing the numerous checkpoints that were manned by Israeli soldiers in Jerusalem and Gaza.

The dreadful feeling that overtook me when I saw Palestinians lining up for interrogation and inspection was overwhelming. How unfair life has been to the Palestinians.

We began our visit by stopping at the Central Bank of Israel in Jerusalem to discuss currency arrangements and other economic issues relating to the West Bank and Gaza. After that we had meetings with Palestinian officials in charge of finance and economic planning who became ministers after Yasser Arafat formed his first government.

I was thrilled to be in Jerusalem. My last visit had been at the end of 1965 when it was part of Jordan. At that time I went there to visit my brother Sidqi who had made Jerusalem his home after he was appointed a director on the PLO executive committee. The temperature was mild and the scenery from my room at the American Colony Hotel was magnificent, particularly the Mount of Olives and adjacent areas. I called Sheila to tell her how impressed I was. I toured the old city and visited Al Aqsa Mosque, the Dome of the Rock, and the Church of the Holy Sepulcher. I also met with friends and relatives whom I had known in Jaffa and Kabul. I rented a car with a driver from the United Nations Relief and Work Agency and visited the Palestinian universities in Jerusalem, Ramallah, Nablus, and Gaza.

During the weekend I went to explore Jaffa with the driver. We started at the Clock Tower in the middle of the city, which was built by Sultan Abdul Hamid II to symbolize modernization during the final days of the Ottoman Empire. Abdul Hamid's efforts to modernize did not prevent him from being overthrown by the Young Turk Revolution of 1908. Nine years later, at the end of World War I the Allies dismembered the Ottoman Empire itself.

Clock Tower Square in Jaffa, 1994

I found the Clock Tower Square deserted and the rubble from the Government House (al Saraya), was still there. Al Saraya was an imposing structure, built by Sultan Abdul Hamid, which housed Jaffa's municipal offices, welfare workers and a kitchen for needy children. One of the Jewish terrorist organizations blew up the building in January 1948 by parking a truck loaded with oranges and explosives near it. Twenty-six were killed, and hundreds injured. Among the dead was one of my relatives,

Ghaleb Dajani, whose father was a well-known Shari'a and civil judge. His maternal grandfather, Sheikh Tawfiq Dajani, was the mufti of Jaffa. Ghaleb together with thirteen young professionals who had graduated from the American University of Beirut, were among those killed. Hundreds were injured, including many children who had been eating at the charity kitchen. All the once attractive buildings around the Square stood vacant and dilapidated.

To the north of the Tower lay Iskandar Awad Street, once a thriving business center. I walked through the street to revisit the offices of my Dajani relatives: Dr. Said (physician), Dr. Jawad Abu Rabah (dentist), Jawad Esq., (lawyer), Rachid (Pharmacist), Hasan Kholki (textile merchant), and Shafiq and Aziz (judges of the court). They and all others in the street were forced to leave Jaffa with their families in 1948. All ran for their lives and died in exile. Their children and grandchildren inherited the bitter feeling of being dispossessed and refugees. All are determined to perpetuate their Palestinian identity and hope that one day they will be able to go back to their homes and land in Jaffa.

To the south of the Clock Tower lay the Jaffa Mosque whose Imam was Sheikh Zaki Dajani a third cousin of my grandfather. He held regular teaching sessions in religion. Opposite the Mosque lay Souk al-Balabsa where shopkeepers sold clothing, perfumes, spices, and other household items. Both the Mosque and the Souk were empty and painfully neglected. I walked a short distance to the Jaffa port and the old city. The sea was calm. There were no sailors and no fishing trawlers. No oranges to be loaded on shipping vessels and no tugboats to pull them over to the ships waiting offshore. I was looking for memories held in my heart since childhood. Instead I saw large and small yachts owned by Israelis. There were no Arab sailors who wore distinct Arab sirwals (loose black trousers) like in the old days. The warehouses where oranges and other exports were stored waiting shipment had been converted into expensive restaurants and nightclubs.

I climbed the stairs to the old parts of the city, perched on a cliff above the port. All the Arab houses had been renovated and taken over by Jewish artists, mostly painters. I looked for a house where two elderly ladies who were friends of my grandmother had lived. My brother Mahmoud and I had visited them periodically. They made sesame halva for us on the little primus stove. We happily devoured the sweets and took some home. The little house had been turned into an artist studio. Really very little remained of the Jaffa I remembered.

I traveled by car a short distance south to my old neighborhood of al Ajami. I could not see our house. I went to a fish restaurant across the street from where we lived. I was told that many of the houses in the area had been torn down and the rubble pushed over the cliff into the Mediterranean Sea; a tourist area was planned to occupy the extended land overlooking the water.

The site of our destroyed house in Jaffa, 1994

The restaurant occupied the site where a four-story apartment building used to stand. All the clientele at the restaurant except for the driver and me were Israeli businessmen.

A number of the Dajanis previously had homes in the neighborhood. I found one home that belonged to one of our relatives. It was occupied by a Jewish family and was being renovated. All the other homes had been torn down or neglected.

I spoke to some Arab residents who occupied what looked like the remnants of homes and asked them what had happened. They said they were transferred from their homes in the north of Palestine to this neighborhood many years ago and they survive doing errands for Jewish families. They also told me that one person by the name of Mohammad Dajani used to work in the neighborhood bakery where he also slept. He died a few years back.

Rubble in Ajami Quarter of Jaffa, 1994

I later found out that Mohammad was the son of one my fathers' fourth cousins who, together with his brother Sheikh Salah, remained in Jaffa. The latter used to wear a white robe and had a gray beard. He carried a rosary in his hand. We followed him whenever he passed by our house on his daily stroll, hoping to hear what he was saying. He was tall, well built and handsome but seemed to be distant. He talked to himself while walking. Some relatives told me that when Salah was ready to go to college he was sent to Germany to study engineering and fell in love with a German woman. He did not do well in his studies and as a result he was called back and when he dragged his feet his father suspended his financial support and Salah had to return to Jaffa. None of my relatives know what became of him after we left Jaffa. He was yet another victim of the disaster that had overtaken the Palestinians.

I retired from the IMF in October 1994 after thirty years of service. In May 1995 I had another chance to go to Palestine for one week under a UNDP project called "Transfer of Knowledge through Expatriate Nationals". On my way to Jerusalem I stopped in Amman, Jordan and spent a night with my sister's family. In the morning I took a taxi to the Allenby Bridge over the Jordan River to Israel, which took about an hour. Upon arrival the Jordanian immigration officer told me I was not supposed to enter Israel through the Allenby Bridge but rather through a bridge in the north. Also, I was supposed to have obtained a temporary Jordanian passport for the trip. I said the UNDP in Jerusalem arranged my travel itinerary and a representative is waiting for me at the other side. After waiting an hour I was allowed to cross.

A UNDP driver was there and we drove to Jerusalem through Jericho over a desolate area uninhabited except for some Bedouin Arab shepherds who lived in tents and who still eked out a living the way they did hundreds of years ago. The driver told me that the Israeli authorities had kept the Bedouins in the area as a tourist attraction.

I spent a few days in Jerusalem at the Palestine Economic Policy Institute and a few days in Gaza at the newly established Palestine Monetary Authority. At the end of my visit I went to Jaffa with Saleem and Marwa Kutob who had become close friends while we lived in Kabul. We visited my old neighborhood and went down to the beach where my brothers Mahmoud and Sidqi and I used to catch crabs.

The next day I went to Ramallah to visit Awni and Salma Dajani who were spending the summer there. At 8.00 PM Salma called a Taxi to take me to Jerusalem. She could not find one because taxis were not allowed during nighttime to cross the checkpoint at the edge of town. The only way was to take a taxi to the checkpoint and walk through to the other side of the street and wait for another taxi to come by if I was lucky. I arrived at the hotel around midnight. My flight from Lud airport to London was scheduled at 6:00 AM, which meant I had to leave the hotel three hours earlier. I barely slept but I made it. The airport was crowded and the lines were long. I nearly missed my flight because of the checkpoints. Life, travel, and work are a hassle for the Palestinians. Taking a taxi from place to place becomes a nerve-racking experience. However, I was very grateful for the two opportunities to re-visit my homeland even though the changes were heart wrenching.

Ajami Beach in Jaffa, 1994

Afterword

Our expulsion from Palestine in 1948 continues to be very painful. Overnight we became refugees. The term with all its connotations hangs over our heads with persistent bitterness but with hope that one day we will be able to go back to our home and land.

My family was able to make a new start, albeit difficult. As refugees we were given the opportunity for employment and education in Syria and Libya. Those Palestinians who could not find employment remained in camps dependent on food rations from the United Nations Relief and Work Agency and other charitable sources. This continues until today. There is a feeling of hopelessness in the camps, a feeling that breeds discontent and anger.

As a student in the United States I was able to work my way through college, and to speak my mind during panel discussions on Palestine or any subject. My American college education enabled me to find employment first at the Bank of Libya and later, after I obtained my Jordanian citizenship, with the International Monetary Fund in Washington, D.C., where I spent thirty years.

Following retirement I was fortunate to be able to get my American citizenship and to vote in the elections. I love the ease of going from Virginia to Florida to California. There are no checkpoints or immigration barriers between one and the other. Residents and non-residents are equal with regard to the right to own property and to pursue happiness within the boundaries of the law. This feeling of freedom is unknown to many in the world today and particularly to the Palestinian refugees.

I have spared no occasion at my work or in my social activities to bring up the question of Palestine and the refugees. I believe that my friends, neighbors and colleagues have become more and more aware of the injustices suffered by the Palestinians and of the need to remedy the situation quickly through an evenhanded Middle East policy by the United States

Government , which is strongly influenced by the American Israel Public Affairs Committee (the Jewish lobby), and by the Christian right.

Since my last visit to Palestine in 1994 negotiations between the Israelis and the Palestinians for the settlement of core issues such as Jerusalem, refugees, Israeli settlements, security, and borders have not yielded any positive results. The occupation continues, new settlements are built, and the separation barrier between the Israelis and the Palestinians in the West Bank has resulted in the confiscation of more Palestinian lands and in the separation of Palestinian families from their orchards and farms, from their very livelihood.

Sixty years have passed since we left Jaffa. During that time my father, mother, and Aunt Fakhriya died in Cairo, Egypt; my grandmother passed away in Latakia and Uncle Ishaq in Damascus, Syria. The next two generations are spread out all over the world: China, Egypt, India, Jordan, Kuwait, the United Arab Emirates, and the United States. We all are hopeful that peace will soon prevail in Palestine and we continue to make a great effort to be together whenever possible to remember our roots and preserve our heritage. Palestine will be in our hearts forever.

APPENDIX A

Recent Developments in Palestine[27]

Major political changes have taken place in Palestine since my last visit.

After his election in 1996 as president of the Palestinian National Authority, Yasser Arafat faced a stalled peace process, brought about by the return of the Likud Party to power in Israel, and by violent attacks against Israel from Palestinian resistance groups, including members of Hamas (Islamic Resistance Movement), Islamic Jihad, and al Aqsa Brigades.

In an effort to encourage dialogue and find a reasonable accommodation between the Israelis and the Palestinians, in 1998 United States President Clinton convened a summit conference at Wye Plantation in Maryland. Some agreements were reached involving redeployment of Israeli troops, security arrangements, prisoner releases, and the resumption of permanent status negotiations. Within a few weeks the Israeli cabinet decided to postpone implementation of the agreements.

The West Bank and Gaza Strip, March 2000

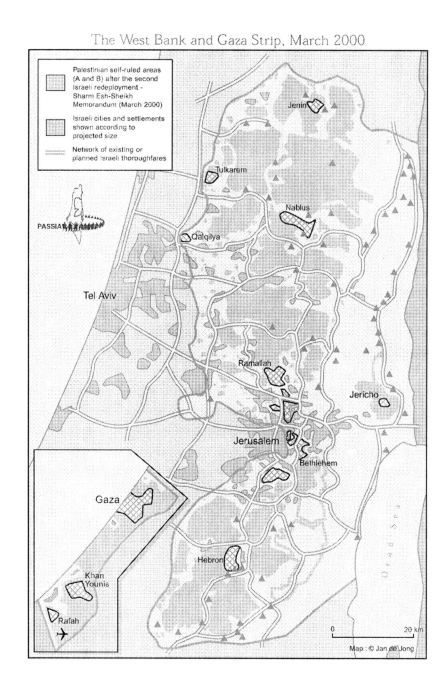

In 1999 the Labor Party won the elections in Israel and there was hope that the peace process would get back on track. In July 2000, President Clinton sponsored talks between Ehud Barak and Yasser Arafat at Camp David but no agreement on the terms of a settlement was reached. A few months later the peace process received a fatal blow when the former military leader Ariel Sharon, accompanied by several hundred policemen, went to the site of the Dome of the Rock and al Aqsa Mosque and declared that the Islamic holy site would remain under permanent Israeli control. This was liable to inflame Palestinian emotions and add to their frustration over Israel's failure to implement the Oslo Accords. Demonstrations and violence broke out in the West Bank and Gaza and quickly escalated into a second uprising or what became known as al Aqsa Intifada.[28]

A new round of talks were held at Taba, Egypt, in January 2001 between the Israelis and the Palestinians to discuss final status issues, including Jerusalem, refugees, settlements, security arrangements, borders, and relations with neighboring countries. Again no agreement was reached. It was later claimed that President Arafat had rejected a generous offer put forward by Prime Minister Barak with Israel keeping only 5 percent of the West Bank. The fact is that no such offers were made.[29] With the election of Ariel Sharon as prime minister of Israel the peace process came to a complete standstill and violence continued unabated, resulting in a huge loss of life, particularly among the Palestinians.

In 2002, the Arab League endorsed a Saudi peace plan based on United Nations Resolutions 242 and 338. However, this plan did not receive a positive response from Israel and violence escalated. Sharon blamed Arafat for the violence and confined him to his Ramallah headquarters. At the same time Israel began building a separation barrier within the West Bank and in the process confiscated more Palestinian lands and divided families from their orchards and farmland, from their very livelihood. In 2004, the International Court of Justice determined that the Israeli Government's construction of the segregation wall in the occupied Palestinian West Bank was illegal. The Court's decision was ignored by the Israeli Government and construction of the wall continued.

West Bank Wall - Map 2006

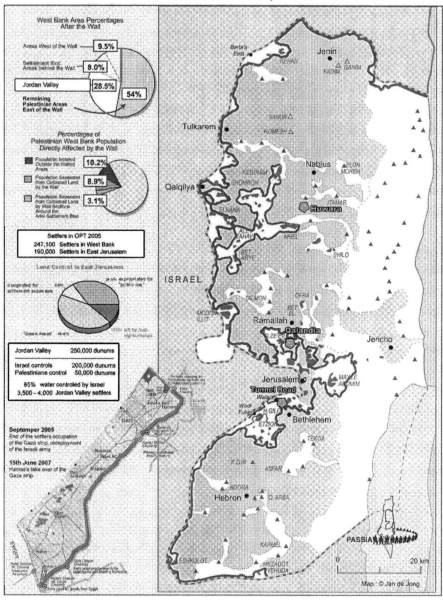

West Bank Area Percentages After the Wall

Areas West of the Wall — 9.5%

Settlement Bloc Areas behind the Wall — 8.0%

Jordan Valley 28.5%

Remaining Palestinian Areas East of the Wall — 54%

Percentages of Palestinian West Bank Population Directly Affected by the Wall

Population Isolated Outside the Walled Areas 10.2%

Population Separated from Cultivated Land by the Wall 8.9%

Population Separated from Cultivated Land by Wall Sections Around the Ariel Settlement Bloc 3.1%

Settlers in OPT 2005
247,100 Settlers in West Bank
190,000 Settlers in East Jerusalem

Land Control in East Jerusalem

Jordan Valley   250,000 dunums

Israel controls   200,000 dunums
Palestinians control   50,000 dunums

85% water controled by Israel
3,500 - 4,000 Jordan Valley settlers

September 2005
End of the settlers occupation of the Gaza strip, redeployment of the Israeli army.

15th June 2007
Hamas's take over of the Gaza strip

Map : © Jan de Jong

0   20 km

Following the invasion of Iraq in 2003 by the United States, the United Kingdom and other coalition forces, attempts were made to revive the peace talks. The "Quartet", consisting of the United States, United Nations, European Union, and Russia, crafted a Road Map for peace, which called for the establishment of a Palestinian state next to Israel by the year 2005. The Palestinians agreed to the different phases of the Road Map but Israel rejected several key points.[30] Violence continued and the separation barrier expanded further. Implementation of the Road Map stalled and violence continued. The step-by-step provisions of the plan proved fatal.

During this period, a non-governmental group of Palestinians and Israelis, headed by Yasser Abed Rabbo and Youssi Beilin, held talks in Geneva with the aim of issuing a peace proposal that builds on the Taba negotiations. The proposal provided for a secure border, based on the 1967 lines—but with mutual exchange of land—a sovereign, contiguous viable state for Palestinians, and a compromise solution for Jerusalem and the refugee problem. Sharon condemned the Geneva initiative, and Arafat approved the process but did not endorse the final text. Several Palestinian groups, including Hamas, condemned the absence in the proposal of the full right of return of displaced Arabs to Israel and the West Bank.

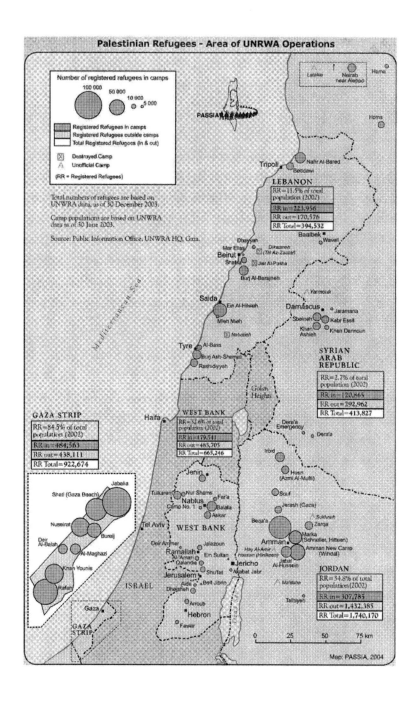

Palestinian Refugees - Area of UNRWA Operations

In late 2004, after effectively being confined within his Ramallah compound for over two years by the Israeli army, Arafat became ill and died on November 11, 2004 at the age of 75. Prime Minister Mahmoud Abbas was elected as president.

The following year Sharon evacuated the Israeli settlements in the Gaza Strip and from four in the West Bank without consultation or coordination with the Palestinian Authority. With no peace on the horizon and with allegations of corruption by Fatah, the party of Mahmoud Abbas, the political field changed dramatically. Hamas, the Islamic Resistance Movement, which had won many local elections, continued to gain popularity and support, and in 2006 won a majority of parliamentary seats in the Palestinian Authority general legislative elections. Mahmoud Haniyah became prime minister. He showed readiness for dialogue with the members of the Quartet and indicated that the rejectionist stance of Hamas regarding Israel could be changed if a satisfactory agreement is reached and is approved by the Palestinian people.[31] The Quartet insisted that Hamas must first recognize Israel, renounce violence, and agree to honor previously negotiated agreements. Financial assistance from Western countries came to a halt and Israel's Prime Minister Ehud Olmert stopped the transfer of receipts of import duties to the Palestinian Authority and blocked entry into or out of the Gaza Strip.

During this period Hamas and the Lebanese Hezbollah captured Israeli soldiers, and Israeli forces attacked Gaza and Lebanon. Hezbollah retaliated by striking northern Israel with missiles, and the war in Lebanon continued until the United Nations approved Resolution 1701, establishing a cease-fire.

In June 2007, following infighting between Hamas and Fatah, Hamas took control of the Gaza strip.

In November 2007, the United States convened a peace conference in Annapolis, Maryland that was attended by President Bush along with Mahmoud Abbas and Ehud Olmert as well as the United Nations, the European Union, Russia, China, the Arab League and other countries for the purpose of producing a substantive document on resolving the Israeli-Palestinian conflict along the lines of the Road Map, with the eventual establishment of a Palestinian state. It was agreed that bilateral negotiations between the Israelis and the Palestinians would immediately be launched to conclude a peace treaty resolving all outstanding issues, including core issues without exception. Let us hope that this time around the negotiations will be successful in bringing comprehensive peace to Palestine and the Middle East.

Appendix B

My Daughters

From left Amira and Zena

Amira has lived in Fort Myers, Florida since her graduation from George Washington University Law Center in 1990. She took a job as a prosecutor at the state attorney's office in Lee County and received quick promotions reaching the position of head of the office in Naples, Florida. She was involved in prosecuting major criminal cases, one of which was broadcast live on Court TV. Amira married Howard Andrew Swett, a colleague of hers, in 1992 in a double wedding with her sister Zena and Barry

Liner. Amira got divorced in 2002. She has two children Alyssa and Drew. She remarried in 2004.

When the State Attorney decided not to run for re-election after thirty years on the job, his deputy, who was Amira's immediate boss, decided to run. Amira actively supported him. He lost the election by a slight margin to another attorney who concentrated his election campaign outside urban centers. After taking office the new State Attorney began a major sweep in senior staff positions appointing new attorneys who were close to him. He asked Amira to resign. Soon she was offered a job at a law firm in Fort Myers, switching from being a state prosecutor into a defense lawyer.

In December 2002, after being in the job a short while Amira at the age of thirty-seven was struck by breast cancer. She felt the lump in her right breast while taking her shower in the morning. Our family was devastated by the news. Sheila and I flew to Fort Myers to be near Amira. The diagnosis was a very aggressive kind of breast cancer called HER-2, in stage III-IV, which required immediate surgery and treatment. In Fort Myers no surgeon was free to do the surgery during the holiday season. Luckily a surgeon in Naples agreed to quickly do the surgery. He removed the lump from her breast but found that cancer cells had spread to the lymph nodes under her right arm, which required immediate removal. In the process he had to sever a nerve in the area, which continues to make her arm sore. Amira stayed in the hospital a few days, and insisted on going to work immediately after the Christmas holidays despite her weak condition.

I drove her to the courthouse where she was scheduled to appear with her client before the judge. The drip bag connected to her breast incision was hidden under her jacket. She did a good job defending her client in a misdemeanor charge. Her boss who was at the court turned to me and said, "Isn't she a great lawyer?"

Amira had taken out a bridging insurance policy after she left the State Attorney's office, as her insurance coverage from the new firm was to become effective after three months from the start of her employment.

Sheila and I accompanied Amira at her first visit to the oncologist. He recommended an aggressive course schedule of intensive chemotherapy treatment: two drugs (Andriomycin and Cytoxin) to be injected simultaneously once a week for three months, then one of the drugs together with a new drug called herceptin for another three months, to be followed by radiation sessions for three months. The doctor told us that the Federal Drug Administration was conducting trials for the drug Herceptin, which works by targeting the HER-2 cancer cells. He said Amira has the choice of enrolling in the trial but cautioned that doing so might delay her treatment if she were selected to be one of those who took placebos instead of the actual Herceptin drug during the trial period. Amira decided not to enroll and hoped that her new bridging insurance policy would adequately cover the treatment. Sheila and I were ready to help. The cost of every weekly treatment was estimated at over $3,000 and the treatment would continue for three months. Amira estimated the total cost borne by the insurance company at about $100,000.

From left: Taher, Sheila, Zena, Mike, Amira, Barry, Kaitlin. Front Row: Scott, Alyssa, Erik, Drew.

Amira started her chemo treatment quickly. Each Friday afternoon she went to the clinic for the chemo injections, which lasted more than two hours and struggled over the weekend to overcome the ghastly side effects of the treatment before she began a new hectic week at work. Sheila and I went with her to the clinic and stayed at her house from late December until early August to help her with shopping, cooking and taking care of the children.

After two years as an employee with the law firm Amira decided to start her own practice. She established a law firm in 2005 in partnership with another lawyer, Steven Ramunni, and the practice is going well and expanding.

Amira has two children from her first marriage to Andrew Swett: Alyssa and Drew, and two stepchildren from her second marriage to Mike Fox: Mathew and Kaitlin.

Zena was very athletic as she grew up, playing soccer, basketball, softball and, above all, tennis. She attended tennis camps every summer. As a teenager she entered tournaments and won many trophies. Unfortunately a severe ankle injury stopped her playing at a competitive level at age seventeen but she still enjoys doubles with her husband and children.

Zena graduated from Virginia Tech with a Bachelor's degree in communication. She moved to Fort Myers to take a job with an employment agency. Her friend from college Barry Liner, also found a job in Fort Myers. They soon got engaged and we had a double wedding for Amira and Zena in November 1991. Zena and Barry moved back to Alexandria where they began new jobs while continuing their graduate work at George Mason University. Zena taught at the Islamic Saudi Academy for three years and now tutors at home. Zena and Barry have two children: Eik and Scott.

Both our daughters Amira and Zena took summer jobs while in college. Amira worked for the World Bank and USAID and Zena with AARP and with a temporary employment agency. Both went with us on home leave every two-three years to visit my parents who lived in Tripoli and later in Cairo, and Sheila's parents in London and later in Hastings where they died in 1990 and 2004, respectively. We planted the seeds of travel in their souls and not a month goes by when we don't hear of another exotic trip they are planning. In 2005 we got together with Mahmoud and Ninon to celebrate their 50th wedding anniversary. All twenty-four of us—children and grandchildren—took a Caribbean cruise. It was a wonderful trip and worth all the intricate planning with some people coming from as faraway as China and India.

APPENDIX C

My Brothers and Sisters

Mahmoud and Ninon had moved from Texas to the Washington area in 1993, which gave us a chance to be together with our children on many occasions. Sheila and I went with Mahmoud and Ninon on several Caribbean cruises and got together for dinner and movies almost every week. Sadly in June 2006 we lost Ninon to an aortic aneurysm and she was buried in Falls Church, near Washington. We continue to grieve over her loss and to miss her daily.

My brother Sidqi and Sana whom we used to visit in Cairo, Egypt almost every other year remained close through the telephone, fax and e-mail. We followed Sidqi's political and scholarly activities regularly. I went with Sidqi and Sana on a Nile cruise in the winter of 2003 and we had a great time together. Sheila could not come because her mother in England needed her at the time. On December 28, 2003 Sidqi passed away as a result of fibrosis of the lungs. I went to see him in the hospital in his last days. We talked about our memories in Jaffa, Latakia, and Tripoli. His hospital room overflowed with flowers sent by his friends in Egypt and other countries. His family received a large number of condolences from heads of state and political and cultural organizations in the Middle East and his funeral in Cairo was marked by a huge attendance. He has left a great gap in our lives and we mourn him still.

My sister Salwa and Ali live in Amman, Jordan. We visited them several times and saw Ali in New York and Washington regularly when he was working as assistant secretary general of the United Nations. Ali has recently retired as the secretary general of the Arab Thought Forum, which he served for three years. We continue to be in close touch and follow closely the news of their children and grandchildren.

My sister Khawla and her husband Tawfiq live near Chicago, Illinois. Khawla teaches part time at Al-Aqsa School for girls, which Tawfiq founded. Tawfiq has set up a successful real estate development business and continues his involvement on the board of the school.

My adopted sister Bashira and her late husband Mohamed Shatta came to Chicago from Cyprus twelve years ago. Mohamed, who was born in the Sudan and had worked as a journalist, sought and was granted political asylum in the United States and his wife and children followed him. He passed away unexpectedly in 2004 as a result of a stroke. We were shocked at his sudden death and we grieve his loss.

How much my parents would have loved to continue to follow the lives of their grandchildren, all of whom have been highly successful and to see their great grandchildren. They certainly would have been very proud of the legacy they left behind. Our journey to America has been a challenge that we have strived to meet with patience, endurance and humor.

APPENDIX D

Retirement

While a student in America and during the thirty years with the IMF I had more or less put aside my violin. The first thing I did after retirement was to dust off my violin and to start playing again. I took two courses in music theory and composition at Northern Virginia Community College, and at the same time started to take private violin lessons from Maestro Billie Anderton who is a retired concertmaster of the Alexandria Symphony Orchestra. I enjoyed my private lessons and our lengthy conversations on domestic and foreign political events, particularly in the Middle East, and on my family history in Palestine. After I acquired a higher level of skill I joined the Northern Virginia Community College Symphony Orchestra and played with the orchestra for a year.

Near our home in Alexandria there is a sailing marina. I took courses in sailing and I have since regularly sailed with friends on the Potomac River. Then came golf, a challenging game that required a lot of training. I took many lessons and have been playing with friends twice a week.

In 1994 I joined the Alexandria Lions Club and actively participated in raising funds for individuals with eyesight and hearing problems in the United States and abroad. After two years I was elected president of the Club and took senior positions in the hierarchy of the Lions of Virginia, including district chairman of the Eye Bank. I have seized every opportunity to inform members of the club about my Palestinian heritage and the story of our expulsion from our homeland, and to discuss with them the peaceful nature of Islam and the war in Iraq and Afghanistan. I have written letters and editorials to newspapers in the United States concerning the plight of the Palestinian refugees and about the root cause of the problems in the Middle East.

I am a member of The Arab-American Anti Discrimination Committee and the American Task Force on Palestine. In my neighborhood I served for several years as treasurer of the Waynewood Citizens Association and of the Waynewood Recreation Association. My retirement years have been productive and enjoyable.

Endnotes

1. Ahmad Sidqi al Dajani, *Hussein Salim al Dajani (1787–1858)*, (Nablus: Dar al Wataniyeh, 1995), (in Arabic).

2. Ian J. Bickerton and Carla L. Klausner, *A Concise History of the Arab Israeli Conflict*, (New Jersey: Prentice Hall, 2005), Chapter 2; Walter Laqueur and Barry Rubin, editors, *The Israel-Arab Reader*, (New York: Penguin Books, 2001), Part 1.

3. Anton La Guardia, *War Without End: Israelis, Palestinians, and the Struggle for a Promised Land*, (New York: Thomas Dunne Books, St. Martin's Press, 2002), 14–15.

4. Nur Masalha, *The Expulsion of the Palestinians*, (Washington, DC: Institute of Palestine Studies, 1992), 75.

5. Anton La Guardia, Ibid, 197.

6. Ahmad Zaki Dajani, *The Tragedy of Palestine*, (Cairo: Dar al Mustaqbal al Arabi, 1999), (in Arabic); *The City of Jaffa in History*, (Cairo: Dar al Manar for Printing, 2003, pp. 199–200), (in Arabic).

7. For more details see Fred J. Khouri, *The Arab Israeli Dilemma*, Second Edition 1976 (New York: Syracuse University Press), 70–75.

8. Palestinian Refugee Research Net, http://www.arts.mcgill.ca/mepp/new_prrn/background/index.htm

9. Laquer and Rubin, *The Israeli-Arab Reader*, 83.

10. http://www.en.wikipedia.org/wiki/Adib_Shishakli

11. Patrick Seale, *Asad of Syria: The Struggle for the Middle East*, (Berkley: University of California Press, 1990); http://www.en.wikipedia.org/wiki/Hafez_al_Assad

12. Bickerton and Klausner, *A Concise History of the Arab-Israeli Conflict*, Chapter 5.

13. http://www.britannica.com/eb/article-22906/Iraq

14. For details see Nur Masalha, *The Expulsion of the Palestinians* (Institute of Palestine Studies, Washington, D.C. 1992); Benny Morris, *The Birth of the Palestinian refugee Problem, 1947–1949*, (Cambridge, UK: Cambridge University Press, 1987), *Righteous Victims: A History of the Zionist-Arab Conflict, 1881–1999*, (New York: Knopf, 1999); Simha Flapan, *The Birth of Israel: Myths and Realities*, (New York: Pantheon, 1987

15. Sunday Times (London), June 15,1969, 12, cited by Rachid Khaldi, " *The Iron Cage*, (Boston: Beacon Press, 2006), 164.

16. http://www.en.wikipedia.org/wiki/Zulfiqar_Ali_Bhutto

17. Laqueur and Rubin, *The Arab Israeli Reader*, 116.

18. http://www.aljazeera.com/news/newsfull.php?newid=10259

19. http//www.en.wikipedia.org/wiki/Yasser_Arafat;
    http://www.bbc.co.uk/bbcfour/documentaries/profile/yasser-arafat.shtml;
    Rachid Khaldi, *The Iron Cage*, Chapters 5 and 6.

20. http://www.en.wikipedia.org/wiki/Liberia

21. Bickerton and Klausner, *A Concise History of the Arab Israeli Conflict*, 171–178.

22. http://en.wikipedia.org/wiki/Mohammed_Daoud_Khan;
    http://en.Wikipedia.org/wiki/Taliban;
    Stephen Tanner, *Afghanistan: A Military History from Alexander the Great to the Fall of the Taliban"*, (Cambridge, MA: Da Capo Press, 2002).

23. Jimmy Carter, *Palestine Peace Not Apartheid*, (New York: Simon & Schuster, 2006) 37–54;

    Laqueur and Rubin, *The Israel-Arab Reader*, 227–232;

24. Bickerton and Klausner, *A Concise History of the Arab-Israeli Conflict*, 224–26;

 Laqueur and Rubin, Ibid, 363–367.

25. Bickerton and Klausnert, Ibid, 250–255.

26. Laqueur and Rubin, *The Israel-Arab Reader*, 413–425.

27. The maps shown in Appendix A are reprinted with permission of Palestinian Academic Society for the Study of International Affairs (PASSIA).

28. Carter, Ibid, Chapter 11.

29. Carter, Ibid, 152.

30. Bickerton and Klausner, 361–380; Jimmy Carter, *Palestine Peace Not Apartheid*, Chapter 12.

31. Carter, Ibid, Chapter 15.

Acknowledgment

Without the support of my wife Sheila and daughters, Amira and Zena, it would have been difficult to stay the course and finish writing my memoir. For years they have been encouraging me to write down my earliest memories so that my roots in Palestine may never be forgotten. From these early memories grew the wish to write about the rest of my life after we left Palestine. I thank them for their support, suggestions and valuable editorial comments. Sheila wrote the passages relating to my mother's cooking and to her family in England and put the final polish to the manuscript.

I would also like to thank my brother Mahmoud and sisters Salwa and Khawla and Bashira for sharing their memories with me. Bashira printed the poem Bride of the Sea in Arabic.

My lengthy and frequent conversations with my late brother Sidqi on the history of the family provided me with much needed information for the memoir. I loved to talk with my siblings about our parents and our childhood together as we moved from place to place.

I am also grateful to my son-in-law Barry Liner for his expert advice on word processing and graphics techniques, to my cousin Usameh Dajani for providing me with family documents, and to my friend Nick Brady who took the time to print my music score.

Suggested Readings

Abu-Lughod, Ibrahim, Ed., *The Transformation of Palestine: Essays on the Origin and Development of the Arab-Israeli Conflict*, (Evanston, Ill., Northwestern University Press, 1971).

Ashrawi, Hanan, *This Side of Peace: A Personal Account*, (New York: Simon & Schuster, 1995).

Beilin, Yossi, *Touching Peace: From the Oslo Accord to a Final Settlement*, (London: Weidenfeld & Nicolson, 1999).

Carter, Jimmy, *Keeping Faith*, (New York: Bantam, 1982).

Chomsky, Noam, *The Fateful Triangle: The United States, Israel, and The Palestinians*, (Cambridge: South End Press, 1999).

Heikal, Mohamed, *Nasser: The Cairo Documents*, (New York: Doubleday, 1973).

Hourani, Albert, *A History of the Arab Peoples*, (Cambridge: Harvard University Press, 1991).

Karsh, Efraim, *Fabricating Israeli History: The New Historians*, (London: Frank Cass, 2000).

Khalidi, Rashid, Ed., *The Origins of Arab Nationalism*, (New York: Columbia University Press, 1991).

Khalidi, Walid, Ed., *From Haven to conquest: Readings in Zionism and the Palestine Problem Until 1948, 2nd ed.*, (Washington, D.C.: Institute for Palestine Studies, 1987).

Laqueur, Walter, *A History of Zionism,* (New York: Weidenfeld & Nicholson, 1974).

LeBor, Adam, *City of Oranges: An Intimate History Of Arabs and Jews In Jaffa,* (New York: W. W. Norton & Company, 2007).

Mersheimer, John J. and Walt, Stephen M. *The Israel Lobby and U.S. Foreign Policy,* (New York: Farrar, Strauss and Giroux, 2007).

McCarthy, Justin, *The Population of Palestine: Population, History and Statistics of the Late Ottoman Period and the Mandate,* (New York: Columbia University Press, 1990).

Sadat, Anwar, *In Search of Identity: An Autobiography,* (New York: Harper & Row, 1978).

Rubin, Barry M.; Judith Colp Rubin (2003), *Yasir Arafat: A Political Biography.* Oxford University Press, ISBN 978-O-19–516689–7.

Printed in the United States
127379LV00005B/10/P